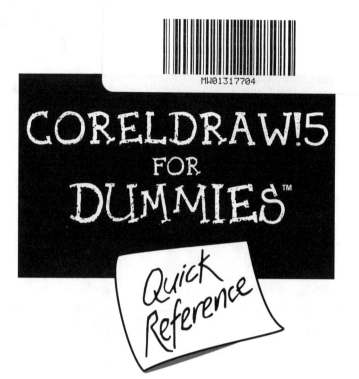

CORELDRAW!5 FOR DUMMIES™

Quick Reference

by Raymond E. Werner

IDG Books Worldwide, Inc.
An International Data Group Company

Foster City, CA ♦ Chicago, IL ♦ Indianapolis, IN ♦ Braintree, MA ♦ Dallas, TX

CorelDRAW! 5 For Dummies Quick Reference

Published by
IDG Books Worldwide, Inc.
An International Data Group Company
919 E. Hillsdale Blvd.
Suite 400
Foster City, CA 94404

Text and art copyright ©1994 by IDG Books Worldwide. All rights reserved. No part of this book may be reproduced or transmitted in any form, by any means (electronic, photocopying, recording, or otherwise) without the prior written permission of the publisher.

Library of Congress Catalog Card No.: 94-79610

ISBN: 1-56884-952-4

Printed in the United States of America

10 9 8 7 6 5 4 3 2 1

1D/RQ/RU/ZU

Distributed in the United States by IDG Books Worldwide, Inc.

Distributed in Canada by Macmillan of Canada, a Division of Canada Publishing Corporation; by Computer and Technical Books in Miami, Florida, for South America and the Caribbean; by Longman Singapore in Singapore, Malaysia, Thailand, and Korea; by Toppan Co. Ltd. in Japan; by Asia Computerworld in Hong Kong; by Woodslane Pty. Ltd. in Australia and New Zealand; and by Transworld Publishers Ltd. in the U.K. and Europe.

For general information on IDG Books in the U.S., including information on discounts and premiums, contact IDG Books 800-434-3422 or 415-312-0650.

For information on where to purchase IDG Books outside the U.S., contact Christina Turner at 415-312-0650.

For information on translations, contact Marc Jeffrey Mikulich, Director, Foreign & Subsidiary Rights, at IDG Books Worldwide, 415-312-0650.

For sales inquiries and special prices for bulk quantities, write to the address above or call IDG Books Worldwide at 415-312-0650.

For information on using IDG Books in the classroom, or for ordering examination copies, contact Jim Kelly at 800-434-2086.

Limit of Liability/Disclaimer of Warranty: The author and publisher have used their best efforts in preparing this book. IDG Books Worldwide, Inc., International Data Group, Inc., and the author make no representation or warranties with respect to the accuracy or completeness of the contents of this book and specifically disclaim any implied warranties or merchantability or fitness for any particular purpose and shall in no event be liable for any loss of profit or any other commercial damage, including but not limited to special, incidental, consequential, or other damages.

Trademarks: CorelDRAW! is a registered trademark of Corel Corporation. All brand names and product names used in this book are trademarks, registered trademarks, or trade names of their respective holders. IDG Books Worldwide is not associated with any product or vendor mentioned in this book.

About the Author

Ray Werner is a freelance editor and author of *Word For Windows For Dummies, Harvard Graphics For Dummies Quick Reference, The First Book of CorelDRAW! 3,* and *50 Ways to Get Your Money's Worth From Prodigy.* In his spare time, he is Adjunct Faculty at Ivy Tech State College in Indianapolis, teaching in the Applied Office Technology and Computer and Information Science departments. He can be reached on CompuServe at 71730,300.

ABOUT IDG BOOKS WORLDWIDE

WINNER
Eighth Annual Computer Press Awards ≥ 1992

Welcome to the world of IDG Books Worldwide.

IDG Books Worldwide, Inc., is a subsidiary of International Data Group, the world's largest publisher of business and computer-related information and the leading global provider of information services on information technology. IDG was founded more than 25 years ago and now employs more than 5,700 people worldwide. IDG publishes more than 200 computer publications in 63 countries (see listing below). Forty million people read one or more IDG publications each month.

Launched in 1990, IDG Books is today the fastest-growing publisher of computer and business books in the United States. We are proud to have received 3 awards from the Computer Press Association in recognition of editorial excellence, and our best-selling ...For Dummies series has tens of millions of copies in print with translations in more than 20 languages. IDG Books, through a recent joint venture with IDG's Hi-Tech Beijing, became the first U.S. publisher to publish a computer book in the People's Republic of China. In record time, IDG Books has become the first choice for millions of readers around the world who want to learn how to better manage their businesses.

Our mission is simple: Every IDG book is designed to bring extra value and skill-building instructions to the reader. Our books are written by experts who understand and care about our readers. The knowledge base of our editorial staff comes from years of experience in publishing, education, and journalism — experience which we use to produce books for the '90s. In short, we care about books, so we attract the best people. We devote special attention to details such as audience, interior design, use of icons, and illustrations. And because we use an efficient process of authoring, editing, and desktop publishing our books electronically, we can spend more time ensuring superior content and spend less time on the technicalities of making books.

You can count on our commitment to deliver high-quality books at competitive prices on topics customers want to read about. At IDG, we value quality, and we have been delivering quality for more than 25 years. You'll find no better book on a subject than an IDG book.

John J. Kilcullen

John Kilcullen
President and CEO
IDG Books Worldwide, Inc.

WINNER
Ninth Annual Computer Press Awards ≥ 1993

IDG Books Worldwide, Inc., is a subsidiary of International Data Group. The officers are Patrick J. McGovern, Founder and Board Chairman; Walter Boyd, President. International Data Group's publications include: **ARGENTINA'S** Computerworld Argentina, Infoworld Argentina; **AUSTRALIA'S** Computerworld Australia, Australian PC World, Australian Macworld, Network World, Mobile Business Australia, Reseller, IDG Sources; **AUSTRIA'S** Computerwelt Oesterreich, PC Test; **BRAZIL'S** Computerworld, Gamepro, Game Power, Mundo IBM, Mundo Unix, PC World, Super Game; **BELGIUM'S** Data News (CW) **BULGARIA'S** Computerworld Bulgaria, Ediworld, PC & Mac World Bulgaria, Network World Bulgaria; **CANADA'S** CIO Canada, Computerworld Canada, Graduate Computerworld, InfoCanada, Network World Canada, **CHILE'S** Computerworld Chile, Informatica; **COLOMBIA'S** Computerworld Colombia, PC World; **CZECH REPUBLIC'S** Computerworld, Elektronika, PC World; **DENMARK'S** Communications World, Computerworld Danmark, Macintosh Produktkatalog, Macworld Danmark, PC World Danmark, PC World Produktguide, Tech World, Windows World; **ECUADOR'S** PC World Ecuador; **EGYPT'S** Computerworld (CW) Middle East, PC World Middle East; **FINLAND'S** MikroPC, Tietoviikko, Tietoverkko; **FRANCE'S** Distributique, GOLDEN MAC, InfoPC, Languages & Systems, Le Guide du Monde Informatique, Le Monde Informatique, Telecoms & Reseaux; **GERMANY'S** Computerwoche, Computerwoche Focus, Computerwoche Extra, Computerwoche Karriere, Information Management, Macwelt, Netzwelt, PC Welt, PC Woche, Publish, Unit; **GREECE'S** Infoworld, PC Games; **HUNGARY'S** Computerworld SZT, PC World, PC World Konyvek; **HONG KONG'S** Computerworld Hong Kong, PC World Hong Kong; **INDIA'S** Computers & Communications; **IRELAND'S** ComputerScope; **ISRAEL'S** Computerworld Israel, PC World Israel; **ITALY'S** Computerworld Italia, Lotus Magazine, Macworld Italia, Networking Italia, PC Shopping, PC World Italia; **JAPAN'S** Computerworld Today, Information Systems World, Macworld Japan, Nikkei Personal Computing, SunWorld Japan, Windows World; **KENYA'S** East African Computer News; **KOREA'S** Computerworld Korea, Macworld Korea, PC World Korea; **MEXICO'S** Compu Edicion, Compu Manufactura, Computacion/Punto de Venta, Computerworld Mexico, MacWorld, Mundo Unix, PC World, Windows; **THE NETHERLANDS'** Computer! Totaal, Computable (CW), LAN Magazine, MacWorld, Totaal "Windows"; **NEW ZEALAND'S** Computer Listings, Computerworld New Zealand, New Zealand PC World, Network World; **NIGERIA'S** PC World Africa; **NORWAY'S** Computerworld Norge, C/World, Lotusworld Norge, Macworld Norge, Networld, PC World Ekspress, PC World Norge, PC World's Produktguide, Publish& Multimedia World, Student Data, Unix World, Windowsworld; IDG Direct Response; **PAKISTAN'S** PC World Pakistan; **PANAMA'S** PC World Panama; **PERU'S** Computerworld Peru, PC World; **PEOPLE'S REPUBLIC OF CHINA'S** China Computerworld, China Infoworld, Electronics Today/Multimedia World, Electronics International, Electronic Product World, China Network World, PC and Communications Magazine, PC World China, Software World Magazine, Telecom Product World; IDG HIGH TECH BEIJING'S New Product World; IDG SHENZHEN'S Computer News Digest; **PHILIPPINES'** Computerworld Philippines, PC Digest (PCW); **POLAND'S** Computerworld Poland, PC World/Komputer; **PORTUGAL'S** Cerebro/PC World, Correio Informatico/Computerworld, Informatica & Comunicacoes Catalogo, MacIn, Nacional de Produtos; **ROMANIA'S** Computerworld, PC World; **RUSSIA'S** Computerworld-Moscow, Mir - PC, Sety; **SINGAPORE'S** Computerworld Southeast Asia, PC World Singapore; **SLOVENIA'S** Monitor Magazine; **SOUTH AFRICA'S** Computer Mail (CIO), Computing S.A., Network World S.A., Software World; **SPAIN'S** Advanced Systems, Amiga World, Computerworld Espana, Communicaciones World, Macworld Espana, NeXTWORLD; Super Juegos Magazine (GamePro), PC World Espana, Publish; **SWEDEN'S** Attack, ComputerSweden, Corporate Computing, Natverk & Kommunikation, Macworld, Mikrodatorn, PC World, Publishing & Design (CAP), Datalngenjoren, Maxi Data, Windows World; **SWITZERLAND'S** Computerworld Schweiz, Macworld Schweiz, PC Tip; **TAIWAN'S** Computerworld Taiwan, PC World Taiwan; **THAILAND'S** Thai Computerworld; **TURKEY'S** Computerworld Monitor, Macworld Turkiye, PC World Turkiye; **UKRAINE'S** Computerworld; **UNITED KINGDOM'S** Computing /Computerworld, Connexion/ Network World, Lotus Magazine, Macworld, Open Computing/Sunworld; **UNITED STATES'** Advanced Systems, AmigaWorld, Cable in the Classroom, CD Review, CIO, Computerworld, Digital Video, DOS Resource Guide, Electronic Entertainment Magazine, Federal Computer Week, Federal Integrator, GamePro, IDG Books, Infoworld, Infoworld Direct, Laser Event, Macworld, Multimedia World, Network World, PC Letter, PC World, PlayPro, Power PC World, Publish, SWATPro, Video Event; **VENEZUELA'S** Computerworld Venezuela, PC World; **VIETNAM'S** PC World Vietnam

Dedication

To Lyle and Lynn, wherever you are. My karma debt is deep.

Acknowledgments

I have been fortunate to have had the opportunity to complete a wide variety of projects for several publishers. Each and every time that I deal with the people at IDG, I am impressed all over again by how far they stand above any other publishing house that I know of in every respect important to an author. The professionalism of their people is refreshing and awesome, and I am convinced that any book I write for IDG is much better than it would have been had this fine group of professionals not guided my efforts.

Special thanks this time go to Pam Mourouzis, the project editor; Diane Steele, fondly called the Goddess of the Quick Reference, a title well deserved and properly earned; and Mary Bednarek, the guiding light of Editorial.

An extra-extra-special thank you to the mysterious Carol Underwood, whose signature on my checks lets me pursue my favorite hobby, eating; Matt Wagner, a really wonderful agent at Waterside Productions; and Megg Bonar at IDG, who let Mary and Diane twist her arm to get me this book.

(The publisher would like to thank Patrick J. McGovern, without whom this book would not have been possible.)

Credits

Publisher
David Solomon

Managing Editor
Mary Bednarek

Acquisitions Editor
Megg Bonar

Production Director
Beth Jenkins

Senior Editors
Tracy L. Barr
Sandra Blackthorn
Diane Graves Steele

Associate Production Coordinator
Valery Bourke

Pre-Press Coordinator
Steve Peake

Editor
Pamela Mourouzis

Editorial Assistants
Elizabeth H. Reynolds
Laura Schaible

Technical Reviewer
Michael J. Partington

Production Staff
Paul Belcastro
Linda M. Boyer
Carla Radzikinas
Dwight Ramsey
Patricia R. Reynolds
Gina Scott

Cover Design & Illustration
Kavish + Kavish

Proofreaders
Barbara L. Potter
Kathleen Prata

Indexer
Anne Leach

Contents at a Glance

Introduction 1

Part I: The Dummies Guide to
CorelDraw 5 5

Part II: The Dummies Guide to
CorelPhoto-Paint 5 123

Index 193

Table of Contents

Introduction 1

Part I: CorelDRAW! 5 Command Reference 5

- Add Perspective 5
- Align... 6
- Align To Baseline 7
- Apply Style 8
- Bitmaps (View Menu) 9
- Blend Roll-Up 10
- Break Apart 13
- Character... 13
- Clear (Effect) 15
- Clear Transformations 15
- Clone (Edit Menu) 15
- Clone (Effects Menu) 16
- Color Correction 17
- Color Manager... 18
- Color Palette 19
- Combine 21
- Contents 22
- Contour Roll-Up 22
- Convert To Curves 23
- Copy (Effects Menu) 24
- Copy (Edit Menu) 25
- Copy Attributes From... 26
- Create Arrow... 27
- Create Pattern... 28
- Create Symbol... 29
- Cut 30
- Delete 31

Delete Page...	31
Duplicate	32
Edit Text...	32
Envelope Roll-Up	33
Exit	34
Export...	35
Extract...	36
Extrude Roll-Up	37
Find...	39
Fit Text To Path	40
Frame...	41
Full-Screen Preview	42
Grid & Scale Setup...	43
Group	44
Guidelines Setup...	45
Import...	46
Insert Object...	48
Insert Page...	50
Intersection	50
Layers Roll-Up	51
Lens Roll-Up	52
Links...	54
Merge Back...	56
Mosaic Roll-Up...	56
New	58
New From Template...	58
Node Edit Roll-Up	59
Object Data Roll-Up	61
Open...	62
Order	63
Overprint Fill (Object Menu)	64
Overprint Outline	64
Page Setup...	65
Paragraph...	66

Table of Contents

Paste	70
Paste Special...	71
PowerClip	72
PowerLine Roll-Up	73
Preferences...	75
Presets Roll-Up	80
Preview Selected Only	82
Print...	82
Print Merge...	86
Print Setup...	86
Redo	87
Refresh Window	87
Repeat	88
Replace...	88
Revert To Master	89
Revert To Style	90
Roll-Ups...	90
Rulers	92
Save, Save As...	92
Save As Style... (Object Menu)	93
Screen/Menu Help...	94
Search For Help On...	94
Select All	95
Select Clones	96
Select Master	96
Separations, Color	96
Separate	96
Show Grid	97
Snap To Grid	97
Snap To Guidelines	98
Snap To Objects	98
Spell Checker...	98
Straighten Text	99
Styles Roll-Up	100

CorelDRAW! 5 For Dummies Quick Reference

Symbols Roll-Up 101
Text Roll-Up 103
Thesaurus.. 104
Toolbox 105
Transform Roll-Up 106
Trim 110
Tutorial 110
Type Assist.. 111
Undo 112
Update Style... (Object Menu) 113
Ungroup 114
Weld 114
Wireframe 115

The Part of Tools and Other Neato Stuff 115

Pick Tool 116
Shape Tool 116
Zoom Tools 117
Pencil Tools 118
Rectangle Tool 119
Ellipse Tool 119
Text Tools 120
Outline Pen Tools 120
Fill Tools 121

Part II: CorelPhoto-Paint 5 Command Reference 123

100% (No Zoom) 124
Acquire Image 124
Add To Selection 125
All (Mask and Object Menus) 126
Arrange Icons 126
Artistic 127

Table of Contents xiii

Build Mode 127
Canvas Roll-Up 128
Cascade 129
Checkpoint 130
Clear 130
Close 131
Color 131
Color Correction 134
Color Manager… 135
Color Mask Roll-Up 137
Color Roll-Up 138
Color Tolerance… 140
Combine Channels… 141
Convert To 141
Copy 142
Copy To File… 143
Create (Object Menu) 143
Create Brush… 144
Create Transparency Mask 145
Crop Image 146
Cut 147
Delete 147
Distort 148
Duplicate 150
Exit 150
Effects & Filters 151
Fill Roll-Up 153
Flip 156
Font… 156
Full-Screen Preview 157
Info… 157
Invert (Mask Menu and Object Menu) 157
Layers/Objects Roll-Up 158
Load… (Mask, Transparency Mask) 159

Mapping	160
Marquee Visible	160
Maximize Work Area	160
Merge	160
Mosaic Roll Up	161
New	162
Noise	163
Open	163
Paper Size…	164
Paste	165
Paste From File…	166
Preferences…	166
Print…	167
Print Setup…	170
Refresh	171
Remove (Remove Transparency Mask)	171
Remove From Selection	172
Remove Transparency Mask	172
Resample…	172
Restore To Checkpoint	173
Rotate	174
Rulers	175
Save, Save As…	175
Save… (Save Transparency Mask)	176
Screen Dithering	177
Select	177
Select Partial Area…	177
Sharpen	178
Skew	178
Soften	179
Special	179
Split Channels To	179
Stretch	180
Tile Horizontally, Tile Vertically	180

Tone	181
Tool Settings Roll-Up	181
Toolbox	182
Transformations	183
Undo	183
XOR Selection	183
Zoom	184
Zoom To Fit	184

The Part of Tools and Other Neato Stuff ... 185

Object Picker Tools	185
Mask Picker Tools	186
Zoom Tools	187
Undo Tools	188
Line Tools	189
Paint Brush Tools	189
Shape Tools	190
Text Tool	191
Fill Tool	191
Smear, Smudge, Contrast, Brightness, and Color Tools	191
Clone Tools	192

Index ... 193

Introduction

Without a doubt, there are 85,492 different books out there about CorelDraw. Each and every one of them aims to teach its readers all about this complex, wonderful, frustrating, and powerful suite of graphic applications. All but this one, that is.

This book answers the burning question, "What does *that* do?" Its function is not to teach you how to use the *program*. Rather, it helps you toward mastery of individual commands and tools. Most of them, that is. If you're one of those guru-level Corelites, pass this book on to someone who's not quite up to your speed, unless you need a prompting every now and again about the function of a particular command. (If you don't, you're probably a pretty boring techno-geek who never makes mistakes, can't get a date, has color-coordinated pocket protectors and taped glasses, and never would have touched a book that had *Dummies* in its title anyway.)

The organization of the book is the height of simplicity. Its main section, Part I, is simply a collection of all the commands in CorelDraw 5 in alphabetical order. The second part of Part I, "The Part of Tools and Other Neato Stuff," lists all the tools and what they do in their order of appearance on-screen.

Moving right along, I then do exactly the same stuff with CorelPhoto-Paint in Part II. Why Photo-Paint, you may ask? Well, simply because I never really saw anything written about it that I liked, and the documentation and on-line help are somewhat less than stellar. So there.

What the funny little pictures mean

Each command has two little icons after it. The first gives you a clue into the usefulness of the command, and the second is my judgement about the safety of your file if you use that command. Other icons scattered throughout the text point to things you should know and lead you to other places to look for more information. The following list shows the icons and tells what they mean:

This guy is cool. He tells you that the command is worth learning about.

This guy is only somewhat cool. He lets you know that beginners may never really have to use the command.

Throw it to the lions. This command just isn't terribly useful, and you may be better served by trying to learn something else.

No worries. Shouldn't offer the opportunity to get you — or your file — into any trouble.

If you're the worrisome type, you may want to be a little bit cautious. You can get into some trouble with these commands, but if you're careful they shouldn't be fatal.

Tread softly. This icon notes the commands that made my system crash. They could wreak similar havoc on yours, too.

This icon points to operations and procedures that may cause disaster or at least minor trauma. Watch out! Back up!

Useful and fascinating information follows this icon.

Introduction 3

This icon refers you to another section of this book for more information.

This icon refers you to a relevant section of *CorelDRAW! 5 For Dummies* or, in a few cases, another . . . *For Dummies* book. Hey, cross-marketing is where the bucks are (and you just might gain something from it).

This icon refers to a new feature in CorelDraw 5 that is not supported in Versions 3 and 4.

Part I
The Dummies Guide to CorelDraw 5

If the idea of using *Dummies* and *CorelDraw* in the same sentence seems a little weird to you, it does to me, too. The fact that you use the program takes you, without any further discussion or proof required, directly out of the world of the dummy and places you firmly in the world of student for life.

You know how you can go into any good bookstore and find those books of notes that tell you all about the classics? They are often so good that you don't even need to read the actual classic to impress the professor with your great insight and knowledge. You can discuss the whys and wherefores of Jason's motivations, discourse on the disability of the Cyclops (he was ocularly challenged), or do any number of other equally fascinating things.

Consider this book your very own *Werner Notes* on CorelDraw 5. This part of the book is divided into two parts: a list of commands and "The Part of Tools and Other Neato Stuff." Use the command reference when you find yourself staring at the computer screen and drawing a blank about what a particular command actually does or how to use it. Use the "Part of Tools" when you find yourself staring at those crazy-looking icons that go down the left side of the screen, and you don't know just what they do.

CorelDraw 5 Command Reference

Add Perspective

Lets you make a two-dimensional object look like it goes way back over there or comes at you off the page. (Think of a railroad track

6 Align...

zipping off over the horizon, the rails getting closer as the track gets further away.)

Using Add Perspective

To add perspective to an object, follow these steps:

1. Select the object to which you want to apply perspective.

2. Choose Add Perspective from the Effects pull-down menu. This action selects the Shape tool and surrounds the object with handles.

3. Drag the handles in or out to mimic the perspective you want.

To keep your perspective uniform throughout your work, see Copy➪Perspective From... later in this section.

For more information about this command, see Chapter 9 in *CorelDRAW! 5 For Dummies*.

More stuff

As you drag the handles, one or two Xs appear on-screen. They represent the horizontal and vertical vanishing points. You can grab the Xs and move them to adjust the perspective.

Align...

This command aligns objects in a drawing. It is particularly useful when you want to keep all your ducks in a row, so to speak. The Align command lines up selected objects by their sizing handles. You can align multiple selected objects with their horizontal or vertical sizing handles in a, well, line.

Digital rodent replacement

Ctrl+A

Ribbon bar icon

Using Align

To align several objects, follow these steps:

1. Select the objects that you want to align by Shift-clicking on each in turn.

Align To Baseline

2. Choose Align from the Arrange pull-down menu.
3. Select the Vertical and/or Horizontal alignment criteria in the Align dialog box.

4. Click on OK.

For more information about this command, see Chapter 6 in *CorelDRAW! 5 For Dummies*.

More stuff

Selecting both a Vertical and a Horizontal option stacks the objects by using the handle that corresponds to the selections as the common point. Selecting the Align to Center of Page checkbox aligns the object and places the result in the center of the page.

If you want the selected objects to snap to a grid as well as to each other, see Grid & Scale Setup later on in this section.

If you don't choose to align the objects to a grid or to the center of the page, the position of the last object that you select is used as the anchor, and all the other objects align to it.

Align To Baseline

This command aligns text to a baseline established by a surrounding text object. You use it most frequently when interactive kerning makes a letter or two stray from the straight and narrow.

Digital rodent replacement
Alt+F10

Using Align To Baseline

1. With the Text tool, select the text that contains the letter(s) that is too high or low.
2. Choose Align To Baseline from the Text pull-down menu.

8 Apply Style

More stuff

Align To Baseline puts all the characters in the selection in a straight line. It does not adjust the spacing between letters.

 To adjust the spacing between letters, use the Shape tool, discussed in "The Part of Tools and Other Neato Stuff."

 For more information about alignment, see Chapter 6 in *CorelDRAW! 5 For Dummies*.

Apply Style

Applies predefined styles to selected text or objects.

Digital rodent replacement

Ctrl+F5 opens the Styles roll-up.

Click the right mouse button on the selected object to open the Object Menu.

Using Apply Style

After you have defined a style, you can apply it by following these steps:

1. Select the object or text you want to change.
2. Open the Styles roll-up (Ctrl+F5) or choose Apply Style from the Object Menu (right mouse button).

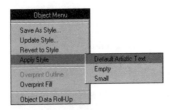

Bitmaps (View Menu)

3. Select the style to apply.
4. Click on the Apply button, if necessary.

More stuff

The three different types of styles are Artistic text, Paragraph text, and Graphic. The styles for Artistic and Paragraph text include Fills, Outlines, Font style, and Size, while Graphic styles include Special effects (envelopes, extrudes, and so on) as well as Outlines and Fills.

See Save As Style... later in this section to find out how to create styles. See Styles Roll-Up to find out how to delete and manage styles.

Bitmaps (View Menu)

The Visible and High Resolution commands determine how CorelDraw displays bitmaps on-screen. They have no effect on how your work prints, but if you're zooming in and out on a complex bitmap or on a page that contains one, they can reduce the time you sit staring off into space while the screen redraws.

Visible is used in Wireframe view only (see Wireframe in this section for more information). You use this command to hide (or reveal) those pesky bitmaps, greatly enhancing the speed of a screen redraw. If the command has a check in front of it, the bitmap shows in all its glory; if the check isn't there, it appears only as a box, a shadow of itself, so to speak.

High resolution modifies the way bitmaps appear in the normal editing view. Draw displays all bitmaps at low resolution unless you select this option. Again, screen redraw time decreases when the resolution is low.

Using Bitmaps

Both commands are *toggles,* meaning that they are either on or off. To make the bitmaps visible or invisible in Wireframe view, choose Visible from the Bitmaps flyout under the View menu. To display bitmaps in high resolution rather than low resolution, choose High Resolution from the Bitmaps flyout under the View menu.

More stuff

CorelDraw does not show bitmaps at high resolution if they have been transformed in any way (with Size, Stretch, Scale, Rotate, Skew, or Mirror). Therefore, you seldom see a bitmap at high resolution, even if you have the High Resolution option checked.

10 Blend Roll-Up

[View menu screenshot showing Bitmaps → Visible, High Resolution submenu]

If you make all transformations of a bitmap in CorelPhoto-Paint first, you can keep the bitmap visible when you import it into CorelDraw.

Using this command can make Autotracing a little easier. Hiding the bitmap allows you to view the traced image and node-edit it without having the original bitmap in the way.

See Autotrace in "The Part of Tools and Other Neato Stuff."

Blend Roll-Up

A blend takes a starting object and transforms it into an ending one, all the while doing some fancy stuff along the way. In this respect, blending is kinda like morphing for the economically distressed. You can change one thing into another, and you don't even need to buy a ton of multimedia stuff. All the intermediate steps remain on-screen in view, so it isn't exactly the same as morphing, which performs all the magic behind the scenes. That's why it's called *blending*, I guess.

Digital rodent replacement
Ctrl+B

The three faces of blend

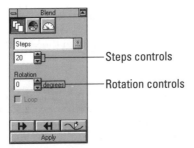

— Steps controls
— Rotation controls

Blend Roll-Up 11

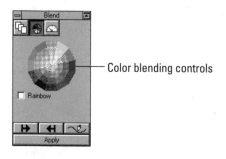

Color blending controls

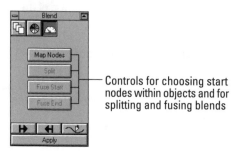

Controls for choosing start nodes within objects and for splitting and fusing blends

Using blends

All blends start with a beginning object and an ending one and can even follow a path you create to get from one to the other. To construct a blend, follow these steps:

1. Draw your beginning and ending objects and separate them far enough to let Draw do its thing — an inch or so is a good place to start.

2. If you want the blend to follow a path, draw that path between the two objects.

3. Press Ctrl+B to open the Blend roll-up.

4. Click on the Steps button at the top of the roll-up box and fill in the number of intermediate shapes you want between the beginning and ending objects.

5. Select the amount of rotation for the intermediate shapes.

6. Click on the start arrow button; doing so changes your cursor to the start arrow's shape. Then click on the start object to select it.

7. Click on the end arrow button and then on the ending objects.

12 Blend Roll-Up

8. If you drew a path, click on the Path button and then on the path.

9. Click on Apply.

If you want to get even fancier, you can click on the color wheel button at the top of the roll-up and modify the range of colors Draw uses to fill the intermediate shapes in a blend. By default, Draw goes directly from the fill color of the start object to the fill color of the end object in a straight line across the color wheel. Selecting the Rainbow checkbox uses colors going *around* the color wheel, thereby incorporating many more shades. You can click on an arrow button to reverse the direction of the flow of colors.

You can use the color blending feature on the shape's outline, too. Select different colored pens for the outline and follow the preceding steps.

By default, Draw searches for the first node on the starting and ending objects and constructs the blend by using these points as anchors. You may want to specify different anchor nodes to achieve special effects or to make a blend look more pleasing. To do so, follow these steps:

1. Click on the button in the Blend roll-up that looks like a little speedometer.

2. Select Map Nodes. The cursor changes to a bent arrow, and the nodes on one of the control objects appear.

3. On the beginning object, click on the node that you want to be the first node (the anchor). The cursor flips over into an arrow pointing the other way, and the nodes on the other control object appear.

4. On the ending object, click on the node that you want to be that object's last node.

5. Click on Apply to reblend the objects.

Yes, you *can* have split blends, and they can be quite attractive in Draw. To split a blend, follow these steps:

1. Select the blend group.

2. In the Blend roll-up, click on the button that looks like a little speedometer.

3. Choose Split. Once you move it off the roll-up, the cursor changes to a bent arrow.

4. Point to one of the places at which you want to split the blend group into two groups and click.

Character... 13

 TIP If you didn't place the blend on a path, you can select the new control point that Draw creates when you split the blend and drag it about on-screen. The original control points stay in place, and the blend reforms to reach the new position. It's very much like pulling on the middle of a rubber band with a string.

More stuff

If you want the intermediate shapes in a blend to rotate around the halfway point of the center of rotation of the start and end objects, click on the Loop checkbox and select an amount of rotation in the Blend roll-up.

Break Apart

Sometimes things just don't work out. The best-laid combinations fall short of expectations. Use Break Apart to uncombine objects that you've stuck together with the Combine command.

Digital rodent replacement

Ctrl+K

Using Break Apart

To break combined objects apart, select the combined object and choose Break Apart from the Arrange menu.

More stuff

You can also use the Break Apart command to assign different fill or outline attributes to text that you have converted to curves.

Character...

Changes the attributes of text.

Digital rodent replacement

Ctrl+T

Using Character

1. Use the Pick tool or the text I-beam cursor to select the text you want to change.

14 Character...

2. Choose Character from the Text menu.
3. Change the desired attributes in the Character Attributes dialog box.

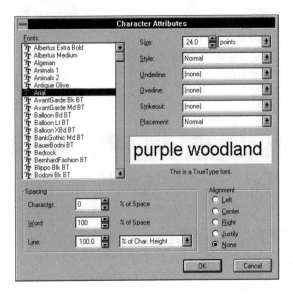

4. Click on OK.

For more information about Characters, see Chapter 10 in *CorelDRAW! 5 For Dummies*.

More stuff

Draw gives you great flexibility in applying attributes. Size can be measured in picas, points, inches, and millimeters. There are six different flavors of overline, underline, and strikethrough, and you can set character, word, and line spacing with great precision.

If you want to change the default text attributes for either Paragraph or Artistic text, press Ctrl+T without any text selected. A dialog box appears asking which type(s) of text to which you want the new defaults to apply. Select Paragraph, Artistic, or both and then designate the new default attributes in the Character Attributes dialog box. You may want to use Character if Corel's default font, AvantGarde, is giving you fits.

Clone (Edit Menu)

Clear (Effect)

Clears the last effect that you applied to the selected object. The command name changes to reflect the name of the selected effect in your document: Clear Blend, Clear Envelope, and so on.

Using Clear (effect)

Select the object from which you want to remove the effect and then choose Clear (effect name) from the Effects menu.

Clear Transformations

This command clears most transformations applied to objects. Use it to reset all rotation and skew transformations, return the center of rotation of objects to the center, reset scaling and stretching, and remove all envelope and perspective effects. It's an all-or-nothing deal, so be sure that you want to clear all transformations before you use this command.

Using Clear Transformations

Select the object or group that you want to restore and then choose Clear Transformations from the Effects menu.

More stuff

Clear Transformations does not clear a Move, Size, Scale, or Mirror effect.

If you select a group of objects, Clear Transformations clears only the transformations that you made to the entire group. If you made transformations to individual objects within the group, you should ungroup the objects first and then clear the individual transformations separately.

Clone (Edit Menu)

Cloning an object makes a duplicate of it and leaves it tied to the original (master). Changes made to the master automatically apply to the clone, too.

Using Clone

Select the object to clone and then choose Clone from the Edit menu.

16 Clone (Effects Menu)

More stuff

Dr. Who, take note: Although the clone reflects changes you make to the master, this link does not work the other way around. If you change the fill — or any attribute, for that matter — of the clone, the changed attribute is no longer tied to the master.

Clone (Effects Menu)

- ➪ Blend From...
- ➪ Extrude From...
- ➪ Contour From...
- ➪ PowerLine From...

This command clones one or more special effects from one object to another.

Using Clone

To clone a special effect, follow these steps:

1. Be sure the object *from* which you want to clone the effect is on-screen.

2. If you're cloning a blend, select both the start and end of the paired objects *to* which you want to clone the effect.

3. Choose Clone from the Effects menu.

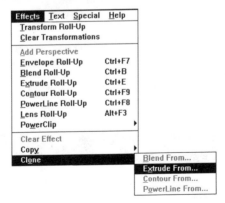

4. Select the effect you want to clone from the flyout menu. The cursor changes to an arrow.

5. Click on one of the paired objects to which you want to clone the blend.

Color Correction

Effects that you cannot clone, usually because they are not in the drawing, are grayed out in the Clone flyout menu.

More stuff

The Clone command in the Edit menu duplicates all effects, while the Clone command in the Effects menu duplicates only one. Changes made to the master are reflected in the clone, but this link does not work the other way around. If you change the attribute in the clone, Draw does not go back and change the master.

Color Correction

- ➪ None
- ➪ Fast
- ➪ Accurate
- ➪ Simulate Printer

The Color Correction command increases the accuracy of the way colors appear on-screen. The command takes its direction from your System Color Profile. None uses no color correction, so it is the fastest. Fast uses some color correction and is a little slower. Accurate uses more color correction, and Simulate Printer, when available, uses the most.

See Color Manager for information about the System Color Profile.

The price you pay for greater accuracy is speed. Unless you have a pretty fast machine with lots of RAM, you probably want to leave this option set at None or Fast.

Using Color Correction

To change the accuracy of your color display, choose Color Correction from the View menu and then select None, Fast, Accurate, or Simulate Printer from the flyout menu.

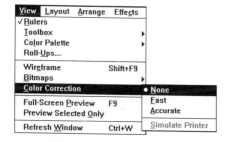

18 Color Manager...

Color Manager...

Creates a System Color Profile for your monitor, scanner, and printer and helps Draw display, acquire, and print colors more accurately. The Color Correction command in the View menu also uses this profile.

 All goes well if your equipment happens to be listed in the menu. If your stuff is not listed, this command is not for the faint-of-heart or for those of you who do not have the manuals that came with your monitor and printer. If you don't have the manual for your scanner, you can calibrate it by using the target image that comes with the CorelDraw manual.

Using Color Manager

To generate a new color profile:

1. Select Color Manager from the File menu. The System Color Profile dialog box opens.

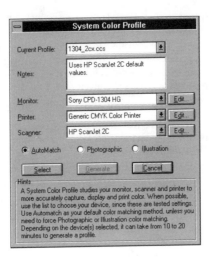

2. Select your Monitor, Printer, and Scanner from the drop-down lists.

   If your monitor, printer, or scanner does not appear on the appropriate drop-down list, choose Other. This option opens a calibration dialog box that allows you to enter information about the device and calibrate it for optimal use in your system.

Color Palette

3. Select the default color-matching method:

   - **Automatch:** This option is your best choice. Automatch determines whether you're printing a vector or bitmapped object and applies either the photographic or illustration gamut-mapping system.
   - **Photographic:** When you choose this option, all gamut-mapping is done by the photographic mapping system, regardless of object type.
   - **Illustration:** When you choose this option, all gamut-mapping is done by the illustration mapping system, regardless of object type.

To select an existing color profile:

1. Choose Color Manager from the File menu. The System Color Profile dialog box opens.
2. Select the profile you want from the Current Profile drop-down list.
3. Click on the Select button.

To edit an existing color profile:

1. Select Color Manager from the File menu. The System Color Profile dialog box opens.
2. Select the profile you want to edit from the Current Profile drop-down list, if not already active.
3. Click on the Edit button next to the component you want to change.
4. Enter revised information or recalibrate the device in the Calibration dialog box.

Depending on the amount of memory and speed of your machine, Color Manager can take a long time to develop a profile — one person on CompuServe reported an instance in which it took two hours to complete. More common are generation times in the 10- to 30-minute range.

Color Palette

- None
- Uniform Colors
- Custom Colors
- FOCOLTONE Colors

Color Palette

  ⇨ PANTONE Spot Colors
  ⇨ PANTONE Process Colors
  ⇨ TRUMATCH Colors

This command displays a palette of colors along the bottom of the screen. You can choose from the four major color-matching systems: FOCOLTONE, PANTONE (Spot), PANTONE (Process), and TRUMATCH. You can also use Uniform Colors for a palette assembled from the RGB model or a palette composed of colors you have mixed and named yourself.

Using Color Palette

To change the color palette, follow these steps:

1. Choose Color Palette from the View menu, which opens the flyout menu.

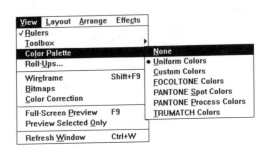

2. Select the palette you want to display:

   - **None:** Removes the palette from the screen
   - **Uniform Colors:** RGB Model palette
   - **Custom Colors:** Named colors, like Twilight Blue and Sea Green
   - **FOCOLTONE Colors**
   - **PANTONE Spot Colors**
   - **PANTONE Process Colors**
   - **TRUMATCH Colors**

FOCOLTONE, PANTONE, and TRUMATCH are industry-standard palettes. Check with your service bureau, if you use one, to see which palette it prefers.

For more information about colors, see Chapter 7 in *CorelDRAW! 5 For Dummies*.

Combine 21

More stuff

The palette displayed on your monitor becomes more exact as the number of colors your system can display in windows increases.

To determine the name of a color (or in the case of RGB Model colors, the percentages of color mix), position the cursor on top of the color in the palette. The color's name appears in the status line (lower-left corner of the display window).

To see more colors of a palette on-screen, click on the up-pointing arrow in the lower-right corner of the palette's display. Doing so opens several more rows of swatches and provides a scroll bar so you can view the whole spectrum (if your system can show that many colors).

Combine

Combines the selected objects or segments into a single object. Draw converts ellipses, rectangles, and text objects into curves before combining. You use this command to combine nodes on different curve objects and to combine objects on different layers.

Digital rodent replacement

Ctrl+L

Using Combine

Select the objects that you want to combine and then choose Combine from the Arrange menu.

More stuff

The most totally awesome and way-cool thing to do with Combine (to me, anyway) is to use it to create clipping holes (masks). Creating masks is really simple to do, as this example shows: Draw a box and then place a symbol and some text (use a fat font) inside the box. Combine the box, symbol, and text and then fill the resulting object with a color or fountain fill. The text becomes transparent, letting the stuff behind the object show through. Cool!

Contents

Displays the CorelDraw Help contents screen.

Digital rodent replacement
F1

Using Contents
Choose Contents from the Help menu. In the resulting dialog box, you can select the general area in which you want help, Search for a particular word, or review the History of your previous searches.

Contour Roll-Up

Places a series of concentric shapes inside or outside the selected object.

Digital rodent replacement
Ctrl+F9

Using the Contour roll-up

1. Select the object that you want to contour.
2. Choose Contour Roll-Up from the Effects menu.
3. Select one of the following contour options:

- **To Center:** Places concentric shapes all the way to the center of the object. The Offset measurement determines the distance between the shapes.

- **Inside:** Places concentric shapes inside the object. The entry in the Steps box determines the number, and the Offset measurement determines the distance between the shapes.
- **Outside:** Places concentric shapes outside of the object. The entry in the Steps box determines the number, and the Offset measurement determines the distance between the shapes.
- **Offset:** Determines the distance between concentric shapes.
- **Steps:** Selects the number of shapes to create. Valid only for Inside or Outside.
- **Pen:** Determines which color is used for the contour outline pen.
- **Fill:** Determines which color is used for the contour fill.

More stuff

If you use the Contour command on an object that has a fountain fill, a second fill color box appears. It allows you to contour one fill color into another.

An object must have a Uniform Color outline and fill for color selections to have any effect. See Color Palette for a description of the Uniform Color palette.

Convert To Curves

Converts a selected rectangle, ellipse, or text object to a series of curves. Once you convert an object to curves, you can edit its individual nodes with the Shape tool.

Ribbon bar icon

Digital rodent replacement

Ctrl+Q

Using Convert To Curves

To convert an object to curves, select the rectangle, ellipse, or text that you want to convert to curves and then choose Convert To Curves from the Arrange menu.

24 Copy (Effects Menu)

More stuff

If you convert text objects with overlapping characters to curves, the places at which the characters overlap become transparent.

After you convert an object to curves, you cannot change it back to text again (unless you use the Undo command). Also, after you convert text to a curve, it no longer contains a character (unless its name is Fred) and cannot be edited with the Text tool or spell-checked.

Copy (Effects Menu)

- ⇨ Perspective From...
- ⇨ Envelope From...
- ⇨ Blend From...
- ⇨ Extrude From...
- ⇨ Contour From...
- ⇨ PowerLine From...
- ⇨ Lens From...
- ⇨ PowerClip From...

This command copies one or more special effects from one object to another.

Using Copy

To copy a special effect, follow these steps:

1. Be sure that the object *from* which you want to copy the effect is on-screen.

2. If you're copying a blend, select both the start and end of the object pair *to* which you want to copy the effect.

3. Choose Copy from the Effects menu.

Copy (Edit Menu)

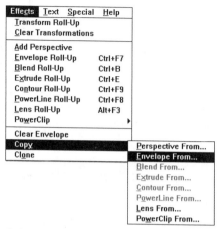

4. Select the effect you want to copy from the flyout menu. The cursor changes to an arrow.

5. Click on the object to which you want to copy the effect.

Effects that you cannot copy, usually because they are not in the drawing, are grayed out in the Copy flyout menu.

More stuff

The Copy command in the Edit menu duplicates all the effects of the original object, while the Copy command in the Effects menu duplicates only one. A copy has no Master/Clone relationship like a clone does (see Clone).

Copy (Edit Menu)

Copying an object makes a duplicate of it and places the duplicate on the Windows Clipboard.

Ribbon bar icon

Digital rodent replacement

Ctrl+C

Using Copy

Select the object to copy and then choose Copy from the Edit menu.

26 Copy Attributes From...

More stuff

After you copy the object to the Clipboard, you can paste it into most Windows applications simply by selecting Paste from the application's Edit menu.

 When you paste an object into CorelDraw from an outside application, it may appear to get lost. To find it, select the Zoom tool and use Zoom to All Objects (the tool on the Zoom flyout menu that looks like my office — cluttered, stacked up, and unorganized).

Copy Attributes From...

Copies attributes from one object to another. You can copy the size and style of the outline pen, outline color, fill, and text attributes, including font, size, spacing, and style.

Using Copy Attributes From

To copy selected attributes from one object to another:

1. Select the object(s) to which you want to copy the attributes.
2. Choose Copy Attributes From... from the Edit menu.
3. Select the attributes that you want to copy in the Copy Attributes dialog box.

4. Click on OK or press Enter. The dialog box disappears and the cursor changes to an arrow.
5. Click on the object from which to copy the attributes.

More stuff

 Be sure that the object from which you want to copy attributes is visible on-screen. When the cursor changes to the arrow, you can no longer use the scroll bars or the zoom controls to navigate.

Create Arrow...   27

One useful feature of this command is its capability to copy just the outline color or just the outline pen style to another object, leaving the other portion alone.

If you find that you're copying the same text attributes over and over, see Save As Style later in this section.

Create Arrow...

Creates arrowheads and line-ending shapes. You may want to try this command with your logo or apply perspective to your initials to make them assume a pointed shape (convert the text to curves before creating the arrow).

Using Create Arrow

1. Assemble or create the shape that you want to use as a line ending or arrow.
2. Combine the shapes (Ctrl+L) or convert the object to curves (Ctrl+Q).
3. Choose Create Arrow from the Special menu. A dialog box appears, asking you to confirm.
4. Click on OK.

More stuff

After you create the arrow, it is placed at the end of the shapes in the Pen roll-up and the Pen dialog box. To access the shapes, select the box that contains a line segment and a down-pointing triangle in either the roll-up or the dialog box.

You can have up to 99 different line endings and arrowheads. If you want to delete one, follow these steps:

1. Select it in the roll-up.
2. Click on Edit to open the Outline Pen dialog box.
3. Click on the Options button under the offending shape.
4. Choose Delete From List in the resulting flyout menu.
5. Click on OK in the confirmation box.

The shape is automatically mirrored from one line ending to the other, which can create an unacceptable result in the case of a logo or initials because one end may be backwards and really hard to read. To get around this problem, create two line endings, one the mirror of the other. Now both ends have an arrow or

28 Create Pattern...

shape that you can read. (Or, if you want to get really obnoxious, you can have both ends of the line display backwards, too.)

It's a good idea to make the drawing that you're going to turn into a line ending or arrow pretty large, say five or six inches long. When applied, it scales itself to the line to which it's attached, but if you construct it on a small scale, it doesn't show up in the Pen dialog box or roll-up.

Create Pattern...

Creates a two-color or full-color pattern fill that you can use for object fills. Patterns you create are added to the those shown in the Fill tool menu and Fill tool roll-up. If you have a small and graphically simple logo, you can use it to create a fill — and maybe even get a raise in the process.

Using Create Pattern

To create a custom pattern, follow these steps:

1. Create the object that you want to use. Anything goes: fills, extrudes, gradients, envelopes, and so on.

It's easy to get so carried away with what you're creating that you exceed the capability of your machine. Remember that it has to draw a pattern over and over again. Simple is good.

2. Without selecting the object, choose Create Pattern from the Special menu. The Create Pattern dialog box opens.

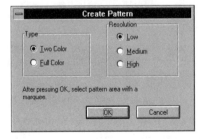

3. Select the type of fill you are creating: Two Color or Full Color.

If you choose a two-color pattern, you can select the resolution you want. If the pattern is mostly straight lines or you're going to make it pretty small, use Low resolution. Use Medium resolution in most cases, saving High resolution for complex shapes and fills. Remember, the higher the

Create Symbol...

resolution, the more your machine has to work to reproduce the pattern both on-screen and to the printer.

4. Click on OK. The cursor changes to a crosshair.

5. Drag a box around the pattern you created in Step 1. When you release the mouse button, a confirmation dialog box opens.

6. Click on OK. If you're creating a two-color pattern, the pattern is saved and you return to the desktop. If you're creating a full-color pattern, the Save Full-Color Pattern dialog box opens.

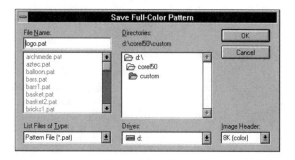

7. Name the pattern, select the drive and directory for storage, and select the size of the image header you want to include. (The image header allows you to see a bitmapped representation of the pattern on your monitor.)

8. Click on OK. The full-color pattern is saved and you return to the desktop.

Create Symbol...

Adds the selected object to a symbol category.

Using Create Symbol

1. Back up your system — all of it, but pay particular attention to TrueType symbol fonts.

2. Select the object you want to turn into a symbol.

3. Make sure that you backed up.

4. Choose Create Symbol from the Special menu. The Create Symbol dialog box appears.

30 Cut

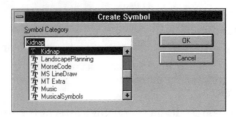

5. Select the symbol group to which you want to add the new symbol. If you haven't backed up yet, you have bunches more faith and trust than I do.

6. Click on OK. The symbol joins the selected category.

More stuff

You must use TrueType fonts to create symbols. After you add a new symbol to a category, it's not easy to remove the symbol. If you back up the font, you can always replace the changed one with the old one. You can also rename the original font, reinstall it, and have both the old one and the new one on your system.

You can also create an entirely new category by typing a new name in the Symbol Category drop-down list. This step creates a new TrueType font and happily adds it to each and every Windows application on your system.

Don't worry about the size of the object; Draw scales it to match the other members of the symbol set.

Cut

Cutting an object removes the drawing or other selected stuff and places it on the Windows Clipboard.

Ribbon bar icon

Digital rodent replacement

Ctrl+X

Using Cut

Select the object to cut and then choose Cut from the Edit menu.

Delete Page... 31

More stuff

After you cut the object to the Clipboard, you can paste it into most Windows applications simply by choosing Paste from the application's Edit menu.

 For more information about Cut, see Chapter 8 in *CorelDRAW! 5 For Dummies*.

Delete

Deleting an object removes the drawing or other selected stuff *without* placing a copy on the Windows Clipboard.

Digital rodent replacement

Delete

Using Delete

Select the object to delete and then choose Delete from the Edit menu.

Delete Page...

Deletes specified pages of a multipage drawing.

Using Delete Page

1. Choose Delete Page from the Layout menu.
2. In the dialog box, specify the first page in the range that you want to delete.
3. If you're deleting multiple pages, be sure that the Thru Page checkbox is checked and enter the last page of the range in the Thru Page list.

 ## More stuff

See Insert Page for information about adding pages.

Duplicate

Creates a copy of the selected object(s).

Digital rodent replacement

Ctrl+D or the + key on the numeric keypad

Using Duplicate

Select the object that you want to duplicate and then choose Duplicate from the Edit menu.

More stuff

If you duplicate by pressing Ctrl+D or by selecting the Duplicate command from the Edit menu, the copy of the object is placed a little below and to the right of the original. You can change this offset in the Preferences dialog box found in the Special menu.

Pressing the + key on the numeric keypad places a copy of the object directly on top of the original. The copy is selected, so you can nudge it about with one of the arrow keys.

Edit Text...

Opens the Edit Text dialog box and allows you to edit the content and attributes of Paragraph and Artistic text.

Digital rodent replacement

Ctrl+Shift+T

Using Edit Text

1. Select the Artistic or Paragraph text that you want to edit.
2. Choose Edit Text from the Text menu to open the Edit Text dialog box.
3. Edit contents or click on the Character or Paragraph button to open the dialog boxes to change character or paragraph attributes.
4. Click on OK.

The Paragraph button is unusable or grayed out if the selected text is Artistic text.

Envelope Roll-Up 33

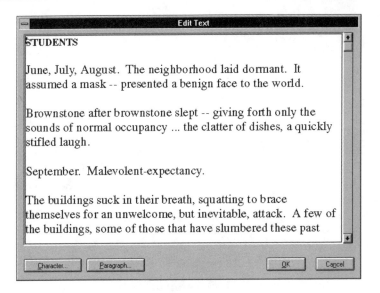

 For information about the Paragraph and Character dialog boxes and roll-ups, see Character and Paragraph.

Envelope Roll-Up

Aside from combines, extrudes, perspectives, and bunches of other stuff, envelopes are one of the "funnest" things in CorelDraw. You can bend and twist an object like it's on a sheet of latex, and you can even make your own shapes to fill with your twisted sister's lyric poems.

Digital rodent replacement
Ctrl+F7

Using the Envelope roll-up

1. Select the objects you want to distort.
2. Group the objects by pressing Ctrl+G (Envelope works on only one object at a time).
3. Choose Envelope Roll-Up from the Effects menu.
4. Click on Add New.
5. Click on an editing mode button:

34 Exit

Straight Line: In this mode, a straight line is maintained between each pair of envelope handles.

Single Arc: In this mode, an arc can be formed between each pair of envelope handles.

Double Arc: In this mode, a double arc — looks like a wave — can be formed between each pair of envelope handles.

Unconstrained: Anything goes.

6. Drag the handles to move the shape about.
7. Click on Apply.

For more information about Envelope, see Chapter 9 in *CorelDRAW! 5 For Dummies*.

More stuff

If you don't feel like making your own envelope, you can click on the Add Preset button to access a list of precreated shapes that you can apply by clicking on them. Also, if you have built an interesting shape that you want to use as an envelope, you can click on the Create From button and then point with the arrow cursor to the shape that you want to mimic.

Exit

Quits CorelDraw and returns you to wherever you started the program (to either the Windows Program Manager or the File Manager).

Digital rodent replacement

Alt+F4

More stuff

When you choose File➪Exit and have drawings open that you have not saved, a message appears and asks whether you want to save your work. To save the stuff, choose Yes. If it has a name, the drawing is saved; otherwise, the Save As dialog box appears. To abandon the changes, choose No.

Export...

Saves your drawing and text in a format that another program can read or use.

Ribbon bar icon

Using Export

1. Choose Export from the File menu.
2. Give the file a name and select the type from the List Files of Type drop-down list.

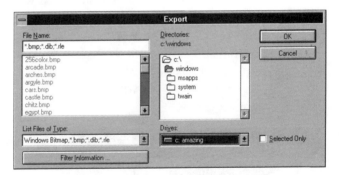

3. If you want to export only selected parts of a drawing, click on the Selected Only checkbox, and only those parts that you selected in the original are exported.
4. Click on OK. Another dialog box opens, depending on which type of graphic format you're using.
5. Enter the necessary information or accept the default options (your best bet unless you really know what you're doing).
6. Click on OK.

36 Extract...

 Watch your file size! You can construct some humongous files in Draw. Many of the Export dialog boxes have an area that reports the projected size of the exported file. It's a good idea to take note of the size before you click on the OK button.

More stuff

Corel recommends that you use the EPS format if you're exporting to a program that uses a PostScript printer. If you're not exporting to print as a PostScript file, Corel recommends the following formats:

If You're Exporting to...	Use This Format
Adobe Illustrator	AI
Ami Professional	WMF
Arts & Letters	WMF, EPS (using Decipher)
AutoCAD	DXF
CorelVentura	CMX
Delrina Perform	GEM (use GEM for PostScript, too)
GEM Artline	GEM
Macintosh-based vector programs	Macintosh PICT, AI
Micrografx Designer	CGM
PageMaker	WMF
PC Paintbrush	PCX
Word for Windows	WMF
WordPerfect	WPG

Extract...

This command saves text objects in the current drawing as ASCII text files. You can then modify the file in an ASCII text editor and merge it back into the drawing. I haven't been able to think of a good use for this command — or even a bad one.

Using Extract

1. Open the CorelDraw file that contains the text that you want to extract.

2. Choose Extract from the Special menu. The Extract dialog box opens.

Extrude Roll-Up 37

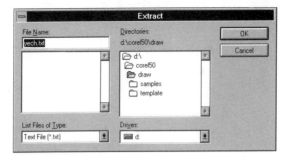

3. Give the text a filename.
4. Click on OK.

More stuff

You cannot extract text that has been modified by any of the following commands:

- ✔ Extrude
- ✔ Blend
- ✔ Contour
- ✔ PowerLine
- ✔ Fit Text To Path

See Merge Back for instructions for putting the text back after you're finished playing with it.

Extrude Roll-Up

Extrudes are cool, boss, far out, and gnarly. They're also pretty complex and way difficult. An extrude takes a two-dimensional object and makes it look three-dimensional by adding surfaces to it. Think of a pasta machine: the extrusion is the flour mixture oozing out of the die.

Digital rodent replacement

Ctrl+E

Using the Extrude roll-up

1. Select the object that you want to extrude.

38 Extrude Roll-Up

2. Choose E<u>x</u>trude Roll-Up from the Effe<u>c</u>ts menu. The Extrude roll-up appears.

— Presets box

3. You can choose a preset extrusion from the presets box or create a new one from the depth box.

4. If you're creating a new extrusion, click on the Depth icon and set the depth of the extruded surfaces.

   - **Perspective extrusions** need values placed in the Depth box.

   - **Parallel extrusions** are constructed by clicking on the Edit button and dragging the X (the vanishing point) that appears on-screen to where you want it.

5. Click on the 3-D Rotation icon, the one shaped like an arrow.

6. Use the arrow icons to spin the extrude about until it looks just the way you want it to.

7. Click on the Light Source Direction icon — it looks like a light bulb.

8. You can apply up to three different light sources, each at a different intensity, to your extrude. Click on light bulb number 1, and a numbered circle appears in the Extrude roll-up. Choose an intensity for this light source from the

slider (or type it in). Drag the numbered circle to the place on the grid where you want the source located. Repeat the steps for additional light sources, if desired.

 9. Click on the Extrusion Coloring icon in the Extrude roll-up — it looks like a color wheel.

10. Choose Use Object Fill if you want to use the color of the object's fill as the basis for the extrude. Choose Solid Fill if you want the extrude to be in one color, or choose Shade if you want the extrude to blend from one shade to another.

 Extrudes take bunches of computer power. If you're using a memory-challenged computer, you may want to pass up shade fills and do the following instead after you choose Shade:

1. Select the desired color(s) from the Using From or To color menus.
2. Click on the Apply button.

More stuff

After you finish constructing the extrude of the century, you can break it apart and mess around with the fills. Choose Arrange⇨Separate to separate the object from its extruded sides. Then apply different fills to the sides and to the object. You can come up with some pretty interesting results.

 For more information about extrudes, see Chapter 9 in *CorelDRAW! 5 For Dummies*.

Find...

Your typical, everyday text-finding doodad. Helps you find text in a document.

Using Find

1. Choose Find from the Text menu to open the Find dialog box (see the following page).
2. Enter the text to search for in the Find What: box.
3. If you want to search only for exact case matches, select the Match Case checkbox.
4. Click on the Find Next button.
5. To exit, click on Close.

Fit Text To Path

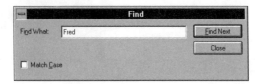

More stuff

Find searches from the insertion point to the end of the document. When you reach the end, a dialog box appears, asking whether you want to continue searching from the beginning.

Fit Text To Path

Takes the baseline of a text object and fits it to a path described by the outline of a selected nontext object. In other words, takes your letters for a ride on the graphic express.

Digital rodent replacement

Ctrl+F

Using Fit Text To Path

1. Select a block of Artistic text (you can only "fit" Artistic text).
2. Shift+click on both the text and the path.
3. Choose Fit Text To Path from the Text menu.
4. Select the desired options from the Fit Text To Path dialog box:

- The first drop-down list in the dialog box lets you rotate characters along the path, skew them horizontally or vertically, or keep the letters upright.

- The second drop-down list lets you change the vertical positioning of the characters with respect to the path. You can align the baseline to the path, align ascenders to the path, align descenders to the path, align to the center of the path, or manually drag the alignment.

- The third option varies with the type of object selected as a path. If the path object is a geometric object, CorelDraw offers a square that has four inset buttons.

  These buttons allow you to select on which quadrant of the geometric shape you want to center the text. If the path object is freeform, another drop-down list that offers you left, center, and right justification options replaces the square.

5. Click on the Place on other side checkbox if you want to flip the text to the other side of the path.
6. Click on the Apply button.

More stuff

Click on the Edit button to adjust the offset distance of the text from the path.

Frequently, you fit text to a path and then want to make the path invisible. No problem. Click on the path and select a line width of none (X) and a fill of none (X).

Frame...

This command sets the number of columns and spacing for Paragraph text. When Corel gets it working, it will be a useful command.

Using Frame

1. Select the frame containing the Paragraph text that you want to change into columns.
2. Choose Frame from the Text menu. The Frame Attributes dialog box opens.

42 Full-Screen Preview

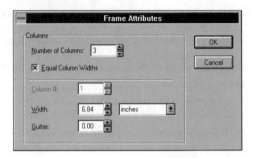

3. Enter the number of columns, desired width, and the gutter measurements in the dialog box.
4. Click on OK.

More stuff

The initial release of CorelDraw 5 refuses to do width and gutter calculations for you. If you really must use this command, you have to do the subtraction yourself. Because the measurements you enter here override the measurements you entered in page setup, you risk making the frame so wide that it doesn't all print. If you have this problem, check to see whether Corel has issued a maintenance release for CorelDraw 5 yet.

Full-Screen Preview

Displays a full-screen view of your drawing. Press any key to return to normal view.

Digital rodent replacement
F9

Ribbon bar icon

Using Full-Screen Preview

Choose Full-Screen Preview from the View menu. Press any key to exit.

Grid & Scale Setup...

More stuff

You cannot edit in full-screen preview. Preview shows exactly how your drawing appears with the exception of any PostScript material (PostScript textures and halftone screen effects).

You can program the right mouse button to pop you into full-page preview. See the Preferences command for more information.

Grid & Scale Setup...

The grid is CorelDraw's answer to the bug zapper. The grid is designed so that such things as lines and drawings stick to it, keeping everything neat and orderly. Setup controls the grid's starting (zero) point, the spacing of gridlines, and whether or not the grid is visible on-screen.

In Draw, scale has nothing to do with union pay. Use scale to specify how many units on the page equal how many units in the real world. For example, 1 inch = 1 foot.

Using Grid & Scale Setup

To adjust the drawing scale:

1. Choose Grid & Scale Setup from the Layout menu to access the Grid & Scale Setup dialog box.

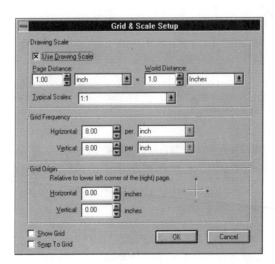

Group

2. Input new frequency numbers and measurements in the Horizontal and Vertical boxes for your grid snap.

3. When you check the Use Drawing Scale option, you can select the Page Distance and measurement. The *page distance* is how much distance on the page represents how much distance in the world; the measurement can be either in inches, picas, millimeters, or points.

4. Select the World Distance and measurement. The *world distance* is how much the page distance represents (don't you love these clear definitions?). The measurement can be inches, millimeters, picas, points, feet, miles, centimeters, meters, or kilometers.

5. You can avoid all the bother in Steps 3 and 4 by selecting one of the presets in the Typical Scales drop-down list.

To adjust the grid frequency:

1. Choose Grid & Scale Setup from the Layout menu.

2. Input new frequency numbers and measurements in the Horizontal and Vertical boxes.

To change the grid origin:

1. Choose Grid & Scale Setup from the Layout menu.

2. Input new X- and Y-coordinates in the Horizontal and Vertical boxes.

More stuff

If you want to see the grid on-screen, click on the Show Grid checkbox. You can also activate the Snap To Grid command in the Grid & Scale Setup dialog box by clicking on its checkbox. The units that you select in Page Distance are used in Contour and Transform. They are also used on the rulers after you change the default drawing scale of 1:1.

Group

Groups all selected objects and allows you to select and modify them as a single object.

Digital rodent replacement

Ctrl+G

Guidelines Setup... 45

Using Group

Select the objects that you want to group by Shift+clicking on them and then choose Group from the Arrange menu.

More stuff

You can select objects within a group to edit without ungrouping them first by holding down the Ctrl key and clicking on the object. You can have up to ten grouping levels within an object. Groups within groups are called *nested* groups, and you can select them by holding down the Ctrl key and clicking, too. (In either case — selecting groups or objects within groups — the selection handles around the object should be round instead of square when you click successfully.)

Commands that do not work properly on a group include the following: Align To Baseline, Blend, Break Apart, Character, Combine, Contour, Edit Text, Extrude, Fit Text To Curve, Frame, PowerLines, Shape tool operations, and Straighten Text.

Guidelines Setup...

Normally, you just drag guidelines onto the desktop from one of the rulers by placing the cursor anywhere on the ruler and dragging a guide into the work area. Sometimes you may need greater precision, and the Guidelines Setup command then becomes useful.

Using guidelines

Guidelines take their measurements from the ruler and are assigned positive or negative numbers by their relative position to the ruler's zero point. Horizontal guides above the zero point are positive numbers, and those below are negative numbers. Vertical guides to the right of the zero point are positive, while those to the left are negative. You can adjust the zero point by dragging from the box at which the horizontal and vertical rulers meet to the location at which you want the new zero coordinate points to occur. Follow these steps to set up guidelines:

1. Choose Guidelines Setup from the Layout menu.

2. Enter the Horizontal and Vertical guideline measurements in the Guidelines dialog box.

3. If you want to see the guidelines on-screen, check the Show Guidelines checkbox.

4. If you want the guidelines to be "sticky" and attract objects, select the Snap To Guidelines checkbox.

46 Import...

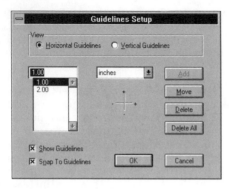

More stuff

Guidelines in the work area can use differing measurements. You can mix and match picas, points, millimeters, and inches without changing the default measurement system used on the rulers. CorelDraw automatically translates one system into the other.

Import...

Brings in drawings created in other programs or merges other CorelDraw graphics into the current drawing.

Ribbon bar icon

Using Import

1. Choose Import from the File menu to open the Import dialog box.

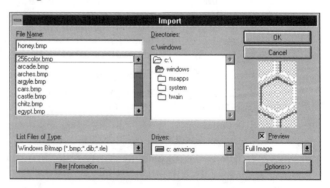

Import... 47

2. Select the type of file from the List Files of Type drop-down listbox. You can often get by with the *.* selection.
3. Navigate through the drives and directories to find the file you want to import.
4. If you aren't sure exactly what the file is or what it looks like, select the Preview checkbox to see a thumbnail image of the file.
5. Click on OK.
6. Enter any necessary information or accept the defaults (which is your best bet unless you really know what you're doing).
7. Click on OK.

More stuff

When you are importing a bitmap graphic (BMP, CPT, GIF, PCC, TGA, TIF, JPG, JFF, JFT, PCD), you can modify the size of the graphic as well as its resolution. Select Full Image in the drop-down list next to the drive to import the full file. The Crop option imports only a portion of the file, and when you select it, a Crop image dialog box opens. Resample changes the resolution of the bitmap. When you select it, the Resample dialog box opens.

You can find Auto Reduce by pressing the Options button in the Import dialog box. It eliminates redundant points in an imported vector graphic file. The value you enter here controls how much variance CorelDraw allows when importing curves. A small value forces accuracy high, but because it results in more points, file sizes are large, too.

Corel recommends that if you are importing from one of the following programs, you should use the file format shown.

If You Are Importing from...	Use This Format
Adobe Illustrator	AI (EPS)
Arts & Letters	AI (EPS), Clipboard
AutoCAD	DXF, HPGL (PLT files)
ASCII text	Clipboard and Paragraph text import
CorelDraw	CDR, Clipboard
CorelTrace	CorelTrace EPS
Excel (Graphs)	Clipboard
GEM Artline	GEM

(continued)

Insert Object...

If You Are Importing from...	Use This Format
GEM Graph	GEM
GEM Draw Plus	GEM
Harvard Graphics	CGM
Lotus 1-2-3	Lotus CGM (more recent versions) or Lotus PIC
Lotus Freelance Plus	CGM
Macintosh-based vector programs	Macintosh PICT, AI
Micrografx Designer, Graph Plus	DRW, AI (EPS)
Scan Gallery	TIF
WordPerfect	WPG

Insert Object...

Embeds or links graphics and other objects into the current drawing. This command lets you include an amazing number of elements in your drawings, blending together spreadsheets, documents, drawings, and a host of other stuff.

Inserting an object can mean using another application to create the object and then embedding it in your drawing, or it can mean plopping an already-created object right into your drawing.

Using Insert Object

To create and insert a new object:

1. Choose Insert Object from the Edit menu to open the Insert Object dialog box.

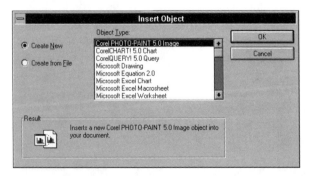

Insert Object... 49

2. Click on the Create New radio button. Applications with which CorelDraw can exchange information appear in the Object Type scroll window.

3. Choose the application you want to use to create the new object.

You open the application to create the object. Some less well-behaved applications may hog Windows resources, or you may be low enough on memory to create a problem when you open an additional application. Moral: *save your work now!*

4. Click on OK. CorelDraw closes the dialog box and opens the application you selected.

5. Create the object in the application. When you finish, click Update in the applications File menu, select OK, or choose Close from the application's File menu (in descending order from best to worst choice.) The application should close, and the object you created is inserted into CorelDraw as an embedded object.

6. To edit the linked or embedded object, double-click on it. Doing so opens the original application with the object active and ready to be messed with.

To insert an existing file as an object:

1. Choose Insert Object from the Edit menu.

2. Click on the Create from File radio button.

3. Change the drive and directory as necessary to point to the file you want to insert. Clicking on the Browse button opens the traditional directory tree dialog box.

4. If you want to link the file rather than insert it, click on the Link checkbox.

5. Click on OK to insert the contents of the file as an object.

Editing the object depends on whether you inserted it as a linked object or an embedded one. If it is embedded, double-click on it to open the parent application. If the object is linked, you can edit it by opening the original file (in the parent application) and making changes. The changes are then reflected in the linked object in CorelDraw.

More stuff

When you link, the object is tied to another application, and you can update it by updating the original.

For more information about linking, see Links.

50 Insert Page...

Insert Page...

Adds additional pages to a drawing and displays a page counter in the lower-left corner of the screen.

Using Insert Page

To insert a page in a document, follow these steps:

1. Choose Insert Page from the Layout menu. The Insert Page dialog box appears.

2. Indicate the number of pages you want to add.
3. Choose whether you want them added Before of After the page in the Page box.
4. Click on OK.

More stuff

If you use the Import command to bring in a multipage text file, CorelDraw automatically adds the number of pages required for the document.

If you're constructing a document in which more than one page prints on a sheet (examples from the Layout tab in the Page Setup dialog box include Book, Booklet, Tent Card, Side-Fold Card, and Top-Fold Card), you have to add additional pages to the document to conform to the number needed for the document.

Intersection

Creates a new object composed of the area where two other objects overlap.

Using Intersection

Select the two objects either by clicking and Shift+clicking or by dragging a marquee box around them with the Pointer tool. Then choose Intersection from the Arrange menu.

More stuff

When first created, the intersection object sits on top of the two base objects, but you can move and modify it without messing up the original shapes. The object created with the Intersection command initially assumes the fill and outline of the last of the two base objects you selected.

Layers Roll-Up

Assigns elements of a drawing to different layers and allows you to create, copy, and delete layers as well as hide, lock, and print them. Layers are for people who really like to get into the nuts and bolts of things. If you love those exploded drawings of aircraft or automobile engines, this one's for you.

Digital rodent replacement

Ctrl+F3

Using layers

Layers are all created alike; they just have different names and properties. So if you know how to do one layer, you can do them all, right?

To make a master layer:

1. Choose Layers Roll-Up from the Layout menu. You see this menu on-screen.

2. Choose the New command from the flyout menu (select the right-pointing triangle to open the flyout menu), which opens the New Layer dialog box.

52 Lens Roll-Up

3. Give the layer a name if you want. I particularly like Fred, but anything will do.
4. Click on the Master Layer checkbox.
5. Click on OK.

This process places the master layer on the page, ready to be worked on. The name that you give to it appears in the Layers roll-up. Because it is a master layer, anything you draw on it appears on every page of your drawing.

For an overview of the Layers command, see Chapter 21 in *CorelDRAW! 5 For Dummies*.

More stuff

Drawings can have a bunch of layers. There's a layer for guides that contains the guidelines you set up, a layer for the grid you set, a layer for the desktop (discussed later), and layers that you create to hold stuff. And you already met the master layer in the preceding section.

The desktop layer is a holding area for stuff you haven't yet included in a drawing. If you move an object off the page area and into the desktop area — called a *pasteboard* in some page-layout programs — the object is available no matter which page of the drawing you're on.

The master layer is designed to hold objects that appear on every page of your drawing, such as a logo, special watermark, or a design element that needs to be consistent from page to page.

You can turn off the display of the master layer elements for a particular page by double-clicking on the name of the layer in the roll-up and deselecting Set Options for All pages and Visible from the resulting Edit Layers dialog box. When you click on OK, the master elements are no longer visible on that page.

Lens Roll-Up

Applies one of eight different lenses to objects in the drawing. Great for achieving special effects. The lenses are as follows:

Lens Roll-Up 53

- **Brighten:** Brightens or darkens the colors under the lens. At a brighten rate of –100%, the colors approach black; at a rate of +100%, they approach white; and 0% has no effect.

- **Color Add:** Mixes the colors of overlapping objects. Objects that are filled with nonuniform colors (for example, fountain fills) are overridden by the color you choose in the Color box.

- **Color Limit:** Filters out all colors under the lens except the one you specify. This option works like a color filter placed on a camera. The value in the Rate box controls the strength of the filter.

- **Heatmap:** Creates an infrared look like that used in the movies *Predator* and *Wolfen*.

- **Invert:** Changes the colors under the lens to their complementary colors based on the CMYK color wheel.

- **Magnify:** Magnifies the object under the lens (think of a magnifying glass placed over an object) by whatever factor you select. The maximum factor is 10.

- **None:** Removes the lens from the selected object.

- **Tinted Grayscale:** Objects under the lens are tinted with shades of the lens color. Think of those old-time photos.

- **Transparency:** Causes the colors of the objects under the lens to mix with the lens object's color, which makes the lens appear transparent. You can enter a transparency rate from 1% to 100% that ranges from no transparency to total transparency.

Digital rodent replacement

Alt+F3

Lens dialog boxes

Using the Lens roll-up

1. Create the object that you want to use as a lens (it must be a closed path) and position it over the part of your drawing that you want to display through the lens.
2. Select the lens object.
3. Choose Lens Roll-Up from the Effects menu.
4. Choose the lens type.
5. Enter any necessary options, such as rates or factors.
6. Click on Apply.

More stuff

The lens object must be on top of the object that you want to display through it. If the lens object isn't on top, select it and press Shift+PgUp to move it to the front.

This feature cannot be used in any version of CorelDraw before 5.

Links...

Lets you view, update, or change links to other Windows applications (using OLE or DDE). This command is useful and worth your effort to learn. If your drawing includes text generated in Word for Windows 6, for example, you can use Paste Special to paste it into CorelDraw and maintain a link between it and Word. When you update the text in Word, it is updated in the CorelDraw drawing. You can create links between all Windows applications that are OLE and DDE aware.

Using Links...

1. Choose Links from the Edit menu to open the Links dialog box.

Links... 55

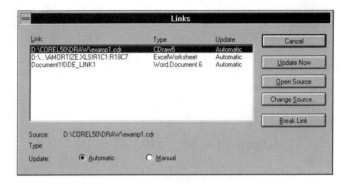

2. Select the linked file that you want to change.
3. Make any of the following changes:

   - **Automatic:** Updates the linked file anytime the file is changed in the source application.

   - **Manual:** Updates the linked file only when you press the Update Now button.

   - **Cancel:** Closes the dialog box.

   - **Update Now:** Manually updates linked files and objects.

   - **Open Source:** Opens the linked object's parent (source) application.

   - **Change Source:** Associates the object with a new application.

   - **Break Link:** Terminates the linkage between the object and the source application.

More stuff

Double-clicking on a linked object opens the parent application with the linked file active and ready to edit. This is a really great feature of OLE, but be sure that you check the amount of free resources your computer has. (Look under About CorelDRAW! in the Help menu and click on the System Info button to see statistics on your system.) If your free resources (GDI) are hovering around 45 percent, you may risk a system lockup if you proceed to open yet another application.

You can insert linked objects into a CorelDraw drawing in two ways: by copying the object to the Clipboard and pasting it into Draw with the Paste Special command or by using the Insert Object command in the Edit menu.

Merge Back...

This command puts the text objects manipulated with the Extract command back into the current drawing. I still can't think of a good use for this command — or even a bad one — but here it is. By the way, if you have an OLE-compatible word processor, you may find the Links command of much greater use.

Using Merge Back

1. Choose Merge Back from the Special menu. The Merge Back dialog box appears.

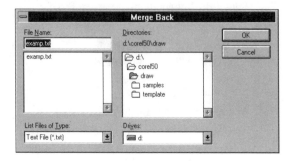

2. Find the file that you extracted and changed.

3. Click on OK, all the while wondering why you didn't do something useful like link it to a good word processor so that you could use a grammar checker or other stuff on the text in the first place.

More stuff

You can't use Merge Back unless you first extract text from the drawing by using the Extract command.

See also the Extract command.

Mosaic Roll-Up...

This is really a neat thing, if it would only support more file types. The Mosaic roll-up is a visual archive of files on your system that can be dragged and dropped into a drawing.

Mosaic Roll-Up...

Digital rodent replacement
Alt+F1

Using Mosaic

1. Select Mosaic Roll-Up from the File menu to open the Mosaic roll-up.

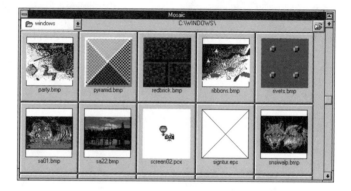

2. Click on the file folder icon in the upper-right corner of the Mosaic window. The Open Collection dialog box opens.

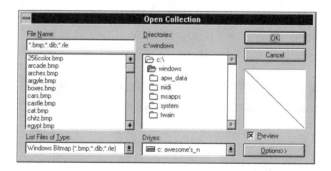

3. Select the drive, directory, and file type in the proper areas.
4. The selected images appear in the Mosaic window.
5. To use one of the images, drag it into your drawing.

More stuff

Pressing the Options button opens up an area that you can use to search for keywords. The Options area also displays any notes that have been attached to a graphic and any fonts used in the graphic.

New

Clears the current drawing so that you can create a new one.

Ribbon bar icon

Digital rodent replacement

Ctrl+N

Using New

Choose New from the File menu.

More stuff

If the current drawing has not been saved, a prompt gives you the opportunity to do so.

The new drawing uses the same settings that were in effect for the old one (Page Setup, Object Fill, Outline, and so on).

New From Template...

You can save one of your favorite drawings, a brochure or card, for example, and use it as a template on which to base other drawings. CorelDraw has defined several of these templates that you may want to use as is or as a starting point for one of your drawings.

See Save As to find out how to save a drawing as a template.

Using New From Template

1. Choose New From Template from the Edit menu to open the New From Template dialog box.

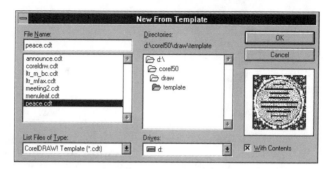

2. Enter the name of the template in the File Name box or use the Drives and Directories boxes to locate the template. A thumbnail representation of the contents of the template appears in the preview area.

3. If you want the contents of the template (text and pictures) to show, select the With Contents checkbox. If you want the new drawing to contain only the settings that are associated with the template (Page Setup, Object Fill, Outline, and so on), deselect the With Contents checkbox.

4. Click on OK.

More stuff

Additional templates can be found in the DRAW\TEMPLATE directory of the CorelDraw CD-ROM.

Node Edit Roll-Up

Nodes are the points at the ends of a line or curve segment in a curve object, or the small hollow squares found next to characters in text objects or along the outlines of objects drawn with the Rectangle and Ellipse tools. These nodes have differing characteristics and can be edited in various ways.

Using the Node Edit roll-up

1. Double-click on a line segment or node with the Shape tool to open the Node Edit roll-up. You have these options:

   - **Add (+ button):** Adds a node at the spot you double-clicked on. If you can't shape the object the way you want with what you have, add a couple of nodes.

Node Edit Roll-Up

- **Delete (– button):** Deletes the selected node or segment. If you got carried away with adding, you can clean up your object by using the Delete command. Also useful for removing those unsightly bumps from an otherwise smooth object.

- **Join (chain button):** Connects two nodes at the beginning or end of curve segments. Use this command to unite two separate paths into a single continuous curve or join nodes on separate curves (you have to combine the paths first to do this trick).

- **Break (broken chain button):** Splits a curve into two or more subpaths. Corel's answer to the quickie divorce.

- **AutoReduce:** Automatically deletes any node that does not significantly change the object's shape. You can adjust the sensitivity of this command by using the Preferences command.

- **toLine:** Changes a curve segment into a line segment.

- **toCurve:** Changes a line segment into a curve segment.

- **Stretch:** Displays eight stretching/scaling handles to let you mess with selected parts of a curve.

- **Rotate:** Displays eight rotating/skewing handles to let you mess with selected parts of a curve.

- **Cusp:** Changes the selected node to a *cusp* node. A cusp node allows a sharp bend in a curve.

- **Smooth:** Changes the selected node to a *smooth* node. A smooth node can have a different curve on either side.

- **Align...:** Aligns two nodes and their associated control points. If you want to align two nodes on different paths, you must first combine the paths.

- **Symmet:** Changes the selected node to a *symmetrical* node. A symmetrical node has the same curvature on both sides.

- **Elastic Mode:** When checked in the roll-up, selected nodes move as if they were parts of a rubber band, moving in a distance and direction proportional to their distance from the base node (the one that you're dragging).

- **Pressure Edit:** Edits PowerLines. When checked in the Node Edit roll-up, a pair of handles appears at the ends of PowerLines. Dragging the handles changes the width of the PowerLine.

Object Data Roll-Up

The Object Data roll-up is accessed through the Object Menu. It allows you to attach information to an object. This information is stored in a database and can include times, dates, numerical data, and text. This is a way complex feature of CorelDraw, and an understanding of database management is a good thing to have if you're going to explore the Object Data roll-up.

Object Data Field Editor

Using the Object Data roll-up

1. With the Pick tool selected, click and hold the right mouse button on the object, which opens the Object Menu.

62 Open...

2. Choose Object Data Roll-Up from the Object Menu to open the roll-up.

3. To manipulate fields, adding, deleting, changing format, and so on, select the Field Editor option from the flyout menu.

4. Go buy a good book on databases (*Access For Dummies* or *FoxPro 2.6 For Windows For Dummies* comes immediately to mind) or find a database guru to carry on for you.

More stuff

Unless you're a database guru or are willing to spend a lot of time trying to understand the terminology and procedures used in database management, your best response to this feature of CorelDraw may very well be a big yawn and movement to the next challenge. If you're a database type, you will spend hours lost in the sheer enjoyment of classifying and sorting all kinds of arcane data about the objects in a drawing, all the while complaining that the drawing just isn't complex enough for you to show your stuff.

Open...

Loads a drawing or a style template into CorelDraw.

Ribbon bar icon

Digital rodent replacement

Ctrl+O

Using Open Drawing

1. Choose Open from the File menu.

2. Enter the filename in the File Name box or use the Drives and Directories boxes to locate the drawing. A thumbnail

representation of the contents of the template appears in the preview area if you select the Preview checkbox.

3. Click on OK.

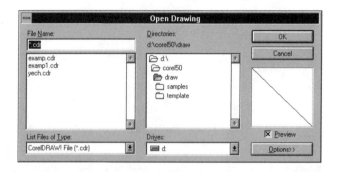

More stuff

You can use wildcards in the File Name box. For example, entering **ex*.*** shows a list of all files beginning with *ex* in the selected directory.

If you have saved drawings using keywords, you can click on the Options button and then choose Find to open a new dialog box. Enter the keyword you are looking for in the keyword search dialog box and then select the Search All Directories checkbox if you want to expand the search to areas other than the current directory. Then choose Search to look through all the keywords to find your files.

Files that meet the search criteria appear in a list so that you can choose the one you want.

See Save, Save As for more information about keywords.

Order

⇨ To Front
⇨ To Back
⇨ Forward One
⇨ Back One
⇨ Reverse Order

Rearranges the stacking order of objects in a drawing.

Overprint Fill (Object Menu)

Digital rodent replacements

To front: Shift+PgUp

To back: Shift+PgDn

Forward one: Ctrl+PgUp

Back one: Ctrl+PgDn

Using Order

1. Select the object or objects that you want to reposition.
2. Choose Order from the Arrange menu.
3. Select the movement you want from the flyout menu.

Overprint Fill (Object Menu)

Overprinting, or printing over an area that has already been printed, creates *traps* (an overlap between adjacent areas of color used to prevent gaps that may be caused by errors in registering colors) in color-separated work.

Using Overprint Fill

With the Pick tool selected, click and hold the right mouse button on the object. Then choose Overprint Fill from the Object Menu.

More stuff

Overprint Fill causes the top object to print over the underlying object, making white gaps due to misregistration unlikely. It is best used when the top color is a lot darker than the bottom one so that you don't create a rather ugly third color.

Overprint Outline

Overprint Outline causes the top object's outline to print over the underlying object, making the possibility of white gaps due to misregistration unlikely. The most common option is to assign the same color to the top object's outline as its fill. Overprinting, or printing over an area that has already been printed, creates traps (an overlap between adjacent areas of color — used to prevent gaps that may be caused by errors in registering colors) in color-separated work.

Page Setup... 65

Using Overprint Outline

With the Pick tool selected, press and hold down the right mouse button on the object, which opens the Object Menu. Choose Overprint Outline from the Object Menu.

Page Setup...

Changes page size, orientation, and color. The dialog box has three tabs with which you can set the page size, page layout, and display.

Using Page Setup

To change the page size:

1. Choose Page Setup from the Layout menu.
2. Click on the Size tab in the Page Layout dialog box.

3. Select the page size from the drop-down list. If you select Custom, enter the Width, Height, and measuring system in the appropriate boxes.

Paragraph...

4. Select Portrait or Landscape.
5. Click on OK when you're done.

To change the page layout:

1. Choose Page Setup from the Layout menu.
2. Click on the Layout tab in the Page Layout dialog box.
3. Select the page layout you want from the drop-down list. Representations of each option appear in the preview area.
4. Click on OK when you're done.

To change the page display:

1. Choose Page Setup from the Layout menu.
2. Click on the Display tab in the Page Layout dialog box.
3. If you want to display facing pages, click on the Facing Pages checkbox to select it and then determine which page you want displayed first.

   If you're working on a multipage document, you most likely want to display the right page first because it carries the page number 1.
4. Select the paper color from the palette. (Click on the color button to open the current palette.)
5. Click on OK when you're done.
6. Click on Show Page Border to toggle the display of the page outline on and off.
7. If you want to add an initial full-size page frame, click on the Add Page Frame button.
8. Click on OK.

More stuff

The Page Setup dialog box's Display tab gets rid of that sometimes pesky page representation that shows on-screen.

For more information about Page Setup, see Chapter 12 in *CorelDRAW! 5 For Dummies*.

Paragraph...

Opens the Paragraph dialog box for formatting Paragraph text spacing, tabs, indents, and bullets. The Paragraph dialog box is divided into four sections (marked with tabs): Spacing, Tabs, Indents, and Bullets.

Paragraph...

Using the Spacing tab

1. Choose **P**aragraph from the **T**ext menu.

   You also can access the Paragraph dialog box from the Text roll-up (Ctrl+F2).

2. Click on the Spacing tab from the Paragraph dialog box.

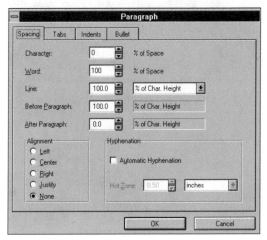

3. Modify spacing as desired.

   - **Charact*e*r**: Sets spacing between characters as a percentage of the width of the space character in the selected font.

   - **Word**: Sets spacing between words as a percentage of the width of the space character in the selected font.

   - **L*i*ne**: Sets spacing between lines of text in points or in percentages of character point size.

   - **Before Paragraph**: Sets spacing before paragraphs in points or percentages of character height or point size.

   - **A*f*ter Paragraph**: Sets spacing after paragraphs in points or percentages of character height or point size.

   - **Alignment**: You can choose between **L**eft, **C**enter, **R**ight, **J**ustify, or **N**one for the text alignment.

   No alignment allows you to use the Shape tool to change the position of individual characters.

   - **A*u*tomatic Hyphenation**: When checked, hyphenates words in the selected paragraph, using the Hot **Z**one to determine how far the end of a line must be from the right margin before the first word in the next line is hyphenated.

Paragraph...

Using the Tabs tab

1. Choose Paragraph from the Text menu.
2. Click on the Tabs tab.
3. Modify settings as desired.

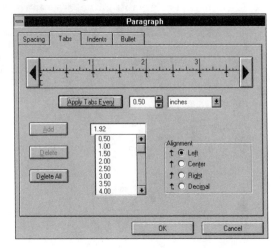

- **Apply Tabs Every**: Inserts tab stops at evenly spaced intervals. Enter a number and a measurement system in the boxes.

- **Add**: Sets a tab at the position you type in the box and adds it to the list. The new tab assumes the selected Alignment options. This option is grayed out until you enter a number in the box.

- **Delete**: Clears the tab stop selected in the ruler or in the tabs list.

- **Delete All**: Clears all tab stops in the selected paragraphs.

- **Alignment**: You can choose between Left, Right, Center, or Decimal for the text alignment at a tab.

You can use the ruler at the top of the dialog box to set tab stops. Tabs can also be adjusted in Paragraph text edit mode if the rulers are enabled.

Using the Indents tab

1. Choose Paragraph from the Text menu.
2. Click on the Indents tab.
3. Modify settings as desired.

Paragraph...

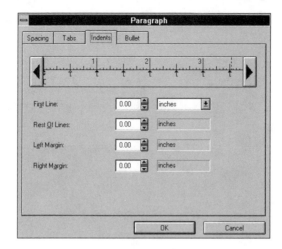

- **First Line**: Indents the first line of the paragraph from the left side of the text frame.

- **Rest Of Lines**: Indents lines other than the first line of the paragraph from the left side of the frame. Specifying a measurement that exceeds the First Line measurement produces a hanging indent.

- **Left Margin:** Indents the entire paragraph from the left side of the text frame.

Bullet Indent replaces Left Frame Margin if you added a bullet to the selected paragraph.

- **Right Margin**: Indents the entire paragraph from the right side of the text frame.

Using the Bullets tab

This command applies a bullet to the selected paragraph.

1. Choose Paragraph from the Text menu.
2. Click on the Bullets tab.
3. Modify or choose settings as desired.

    - **Bullet On:** Check to apply the bullet to the selected paragraph.

    - **Symbol #:** After you choose the symbol set from the scroll list, you can enter the index number of a symbol from the Symbol and Clipart Catalog to immediately display it.

    - **Category scroll box:** Lists the various symbol sets.

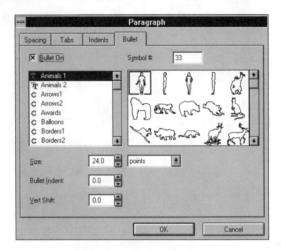

- **Symbols scroll box:** Displays symbols in the selected category. Click on the one you want to use and drag it into the drawing or double-click to bring it in.

- **Size:** Specifies the size of the bullet. Although CorelDraw sizes the bullet in proportion to the text, you can specify another size here.

- **Bullet Indent:** Specifies the distance between the bullet and the left side of the text frame.

- **Vertical Shift:** Shifts the bullet up or down.

After adding the bullet, you can select it with the Text or Shape tool and change its size, fill, and outline.

More stuff

Choosing the Paragraph command with either no text or at least two text objects selected lets you change the default Artistic and/or Paragraph text styles.

Paste

Pastes Clipboard contents into a drawing.

Digital rodent replacement

Ctrl+V

Ribbon bar icon

Paste Special... 71

Using Paste

Be sure that the object you want to paste into CorelDraw is on the Clipboard. Then choose Paste from the Edit menu.

More stuff

Objects that are pasted from other CorelDraw drawings are most often pasted into the current drawing at the same location that they had in the original. Objects pasted from other applications tend to be placed in the center of the current drawing.

 If you can't find the object after it has been placed, it may be located in an area that is not displayed on-screen. Choose the Zoom tool and click on the Show All Objects icon from the flyout menu (it's the one that looks like stacked shapes). This command expands the view of the drawing to show all objects. After you zoom to show all the objects, the new pasted object is the only object selected on-screen.

Paste Special...

Pastes Clipboard contents into a drawing and allows you to specify the format of the information and create a link to the source file.

Using Paste Special

1. Be sure that the information you want to paste is on the Windows Clipboard (see Cut and Copy).

2. From the Edit menu, choose Paste Special, which opens the Paste Special dialog box.

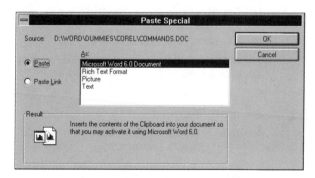

3. Make selections in the dialog box.

PowerClip

- The **Source** area displays the name and location of the source file providing the information.

- Selecting the **Paste** radio button inserts the contents of the Clipboard into the drawing without creating a link to the source file.

- Selecting **Paste Link** inserts the contents of the Clipboard and creates a link to the source file.

The Paste Link option is available only if the Clipboard contents came from an application that can link information to CorelDraw.

- **As** lets you choose which format you want to use. Several programs allow you to use differing formats of information, like RTF or ASCII.

PowerClip

⇨ Place Inside Container...
⇨ Extract Contents
⇨ Edit Contents
⇨ Finish Editing This Level

Places an object inside another object. This command is one of the most excellent additions to CorelDraw 5. You can use Artistic text, grouped objects, and closed paths as both container and contents objects. Bitmaps and Paragraph text are limited to contents objects.

The container object acts as a frame. Contents objects placed inside the container appear only within the boundaries of the container. You can rotate, resize, and stretch the whole PowerClip object or only the container or contents object.

Using PowerClip

To place an object inside a container:

1. Construct the container object and import or construct the contents object.
2. Select the contents object.
3. Choose PowerClip from the Effects menu.
4. Choose Place Inside Container from the submenu. The cursor changes to an arrow.
5. Click on the container object. The contents object is placed within the container object.

To adjust the position of the contents object within the container:

PowerLine Roll-Up

1. Select the PowerClip object.
2. Choose PoweClip from the Effects menu.

3. Choose Edit Contents from the submenu. The entire contents object becomes visible, and the container object changes to blue lines.
4. Drag the contents object to a new position relative to the container or use the arrow keys to nudge it into the proper position.
5. Choose Finish Editing This Level from the PowerClip submenu to end your repositioning.

To extract the contents of a PowerClip, follow these steps:

1. Select the PowerClip object.
2. Choose PoweClip from the Effects menu.
3. Choose Extract Contents from the submenu.

More stuff

By default, a contents object is centered inside a container object. You can change this default by disabling the Auto-Center Place Inside option in the Preferences⇨General dialog box (see Preferences).

You can use a PowerClip object as a contents object and place it inside a container, creating a nested PowerClip. You can continue this for up to five levels. Selecting the PowerClip and then choosing the PowerClip⇨Edit Contents command lets you move through the nested levels.

PowerLine Roll-Up

Lets you select from a variety of pen shapes and effects to give your drawing that handmade, down-home look. Allows you to draw lines of varying thickness.

PowerLine Roll-Up

Digital rodent replacement

Ctrl+F8

Using the PowerLine roll-up

1. Choose PowerLine Roll-Up from the Effects menu to access the roll-up.

2. Select the line you want to use from the presets listbox. A representation of the shape appears in the viewing area.

3. Specify the maximum width of the PowerLine in the Max Width box.

4. Click on the Apply when drawing lines checkbox if you want all lines drawn with the Pencil tool to be PowerLines.

5. Click on the Pen button to get at the controls for changing the shape and angle of the nib.

6. Click on the Speedometer button to access the controls for changing the width of the line as it changes direction (Speed), adjusting the smoothness of the line (Spread), and varying the amount of ink used as the line gets thinner and fatter (Ink Flow).

7. If you want the proportions of the PowerLine to stay in scale with the object, select the Scale with Image checkbox.

8. Select the Pencil tool and draw away.

More stuff

You can use the PowerLine effect to outline existing objects by selecting the object and applying a PowerLine to it. PowerLines can be manipulated with the Shape tool, and the Node Edit roll-up can also modify the effect.

Preferences...

Allows you to set a multitude of options that affect the way CorelDraw displays objects and performs certain operations. The dialog box contains five tabs called General, Curves, Text, View, and Advanced.

Digital rodent replacement

Ctrl+J

Using Preferences

Choose Preferences from the Special menu and then make modifications to the selected tab.

General tab

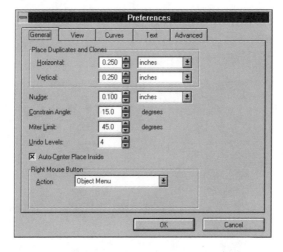

- **Place Duplicates and Clones:** Controls how far away from the original or master a duplicate or clone is placed. Enter desired distance and measurements in the Horizontal and Vertical boxes.

- **Nudge:** Controls how far a selected object moves when you press the direction keys. The maximum movement is 2 inches or its equivalent. The minimum is 1/1000 of an inch, 1/10 of a millimeter or point, or 0,1 if you're using the picas, point measurement.

Preferences...

- **Constrain Angle:** Controls the angle of motion when you press the Ctrl key while skewing or rotating, drawing straight lines in Freehand mode, or adjusting control points in Bezier mode.

- **Miter Limit:** All corners that are less than the selected limit have a beveled point, and corners that are above the limit come to a sharp point.

- **Undo Levels:** Sets the number of actions that you can undo with the Edit⇨Undo command.

The greater the number of undo levels you select, the more memory CorelDraw needs to run.

- **Auto-Center Place Inside:** Determines whether PowerClip contents are centered in the container object automatically.

- **Right Mouse Button:** Selects the Action that is assigned to the right mouse button.

If you assign an Action to the right mouse button, you must keep the button depressed for a second or so if you want to access the Object Menu.

View tab

- **Auto Panning:** When this option is selected, the window scrolls when you attempt to drag beyond its borders.

- **Interruptible Refresh:** Lets you interrupt a screen redraw by clicking or pressing a key.

Preferences...

- **Manual Refresh:** Lets you redraw the screen by clicking on one of the scroll bars or by using the Refresh Window command in the View window.

- **Cross Hair Cursor:** Turns the mouse pointer into crosshairs while in the drawing area.

- **Preview Fountain Steps:** Determines the number of bands that represent fountain fills on-screen or in objects exported in AI, EPS, CGM, PCT, WMF, or bitmapped formats.

  The least amount of fountain steps provides a faster preview.

- **Draw When Moving:** Displays objects on-screen as you move them. Takes lots of memory and time.

- **Delay to Draw When Moving:** Tells CorelDraw how long to wait before starting to draw the moving object.

- **Show Status Line:** Duh, yup, which way did he go?

  - **Place On Top:** Puts the status line at the top of the drawing window (Versions 1, 2, 3, and 4 are this way).

  - **Place On Bottom:** See if you can guess (the default in Version 5).

  - **Small Size:** Reduces the size of the status line and eliminates the selected object's sizing information.

- **Show Menu & Tool Help:** Displays or hides those helpful messages and pop-up tool descriptions in the status line.

- **Show Ribbon Bar:** Shows or hides the ribbon bar.

- **Show Pop-Up Help:** Shows or hides that sometimes obnoxious pop-up help stuff.

Curves tab

- **Freehand Tracking:** Controls how closely the motion of the mouse is followed when drawing in Freehand mode. Lower numbers tend to give rougher results.

- **Autotrace Tracking:** Controls how closely the edges of a bitmap are traced when using Autotrace. Lower numbers (1 to 3) tend to give more accurate results, but the tracing line contains many nodes, making it harder to edit.

- **Corner Threshold:** When you're drawing in Freehand mode, corners are either smooth or cusps. The lower this number is set, the more apt CorelDraw is to interpret a corner as a cusp.

Preferences...

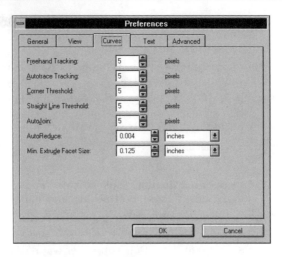

- **Straight Line Threshold:** When you're drawing in Freehand mode, lines are either straight or curve segments. The lower this number is set, the more apt CorelDraw is to interpret a line as a curve.

- **Auto-Join:** Controls how far apart two nodes can be and still be joined when drawing in Freehand or Bezier mode.

- **AutoReduce:** Controls how many nodes are offed when you use the AutoReduce option in the Node Edit roll-up. The higher the setting, the more nodes are removed.

- **Minimum Extrude Facet Size:** Changes the facet size (the distance between shades of color in extrusions) when CorelDraw is displaying or printing drawings that contain extrusions. Lower numbers (0.01 – 0.1) give better results but take more time to draw and print.

Text tab

- **Edit Text on Screen:** Toggles to allow text editing to happen on-screen or only in the Text dialog box.

- **Show Font Sample in Text roll-up:** Toggles the sample in the roll-up.

- **Minimum Line Width:** Sets the minimum number of characters that CorelDraw places on a line in an envelope. (This applies only to Paragraph text.)

- **Greek Text Below:** Translates text into squiggly lines below the specified size. Screen redraw is faster when this value is set to a high number.

Preferences... 79

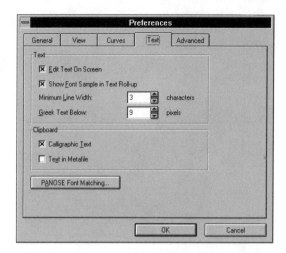

- ✔ **Calligraphic Text:** Specifies whether calligraphic pen outlines are placed on the Clipboard or exported with one of the vector export filters.

- ✔ **Text in Metafile:** When checked, text is exported with its font, point size, and other attributes intact. When deselected, text is exported as curves.

- ✔ **PANOSE Font Matching:** New to Version 5, this option allows CorelDraw to take its best guess at fonts that may be in imported files but are not on your system. Clicking on this button opens another dialog box that allows you to enable or disable Font Matching, show the names of missing fonts and the replacement font used by CorelDraw, determine how exact the font match must be, select the default font to be used if CorelDraw can't even take a good guess, list alternative spellings for font names, or stipulate a particular font to be used as a substitute for another one.

Although PANOSE Font Matching is a great thing, it doesn't work on the files that you have opened or imported by using the neato drag-and-drop feature of OLE2.

Advanced tab

- ✔ **Backup:** You can create backup files when saving, and you can make automatic backups at set intervals with this option. Click on the Select Directory button to tell CorelDraw where to place the backup files.

People have a tendency to disable automatic backups because they are a pain — especially when you're in the middle of something and the system decides to make you

Presets Roll-Up

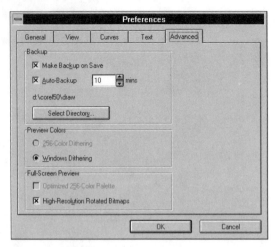

stop so that it can back up the stuff. If you have disabled Backup, be aware that your work is at risk. Be safe and press Ctrl+S often.

- ✔ **Preview Colors:** Controls how colors are displayed on-screen. 256-Color Dithering uses CorelDraw's color mixing scheme. Windows Dithering uses the dithering scheme of the Window's screen driver.

- ✔ **Full-Screen Preview:** Optimized 256-Color Palette loads the palette with pure colors. High-Resolution Rotated Bitmaps, when selected, displays rotated bitmaps at full resolution. This takes time and memory. Disable this option if you want to speed up screen refresh rates.

Presets Roll-Up

Allows you to create, store, and use bunches of preset effects, such as 3-D images, drop shadows, and wonderful fountain fills. It also gives you access to many prebuilt effects, some of which are totally awesome.

Digital rodent replacement

Alt+F5

Using the Presets roll-up

If you are attempting to apply an effect to text and the Apply button is grayed out, try converting the text to curves.

Presets Roll-Up 81

To apply one of the built-in presets:

1. Select the object or text to which you want to apply the preset.
2. Choose Presets Roll-Up from the Special menu.
3. Select the preset you want from the drop-down list. (A thumbnail representation of the effect appears in the top of the dialog box, and any notes that you have attached become visible.)

4. Click on the Apply button.

To add notes or delete a preset from the drop-down list:

1. Choose Presets Roll-Up from the Special menu.
2. Select the preset you want to edit from the drop-down list.
3. Choose Edit, which opens another dialog box where you can enter notes or delete the preset by clicking on the Delete button and then selecting the presets you want to delete from the resulting dialog box.

To build your own preset:

1. Select the unadorned object.
2. Choose Presets Roll-Up from the Special menu.
3. Choose Start Recording.
4. Make any of the following modifications: Move, Stretch, Skew, Rotate, Fill, Outline, Duplicate, To Front, To Back, Forward One, Back One, or Convert To Curves.
5. Choose Stop Recording, which opens the Edit dialog box.
6. Give your new creation a name and attach notes.
7. Click on OK.

More stuff

This command is so much fun and so absorbing that it can lead to sleepless nights and fights with your spouse. Try the Ice on Chrome preset — mondo magnifico, fer sure.

Preview Selected Only

Preview Selected Only

Allows you to toggle between viewing everything in Full Screen Preview mode and viewing just the selected objects.

Using Preview Selected Only

Choose Preview Selected Only from the View menu. When this option is checked, only the selected objects appear in Full Screen Preview mode (F9). When it is unchecked, the entire drawing appears.

More stuff

If you use full-screen preview, this command can dramatically reduce screen redraw time. Unfortunately, it doesn't do anything for the normal view redraw.

To speed up the redraw time under normal circumstances, see Wireframe later in this section.

Print...

Lets you print all or part of your document. You have a ton of different selections for the way your document prints: color separations, reference marks, layout, and more.

Digital rodent replacement

Ctrl+P

Ribbon bar icon

Using Print

1. Choose Print from the File menu.
2. Select desired options in the Print dialog box:
   - **All:** Prints the whole banana.
   - **Selected Objects:** Prints only the selected objects.
   - **Current Page:** Prints only the page in the view window.

Print... 83

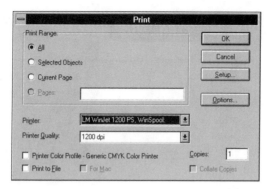

- **Pages:** Specify the range of pages you want to print — separate individual pages with a comma or stipulate a range in the form 3–5. You can mix and match, too: **1–3,4,7,45** prints pages 1, 2, 3, 4, 7, and 45.

  If you want to print every other page, use the tilde (~). Telling CorelDraw to print 1~ results in all odd-numbered pages printing, 2~ prints all even-numbered pages, and 1~13 prints all odd-numbered pages between 1 and 13.

- **Printer:** Shows the active printer. Choose any installed printer from the drop-down list.

- **Printer Quality:** Choose the resolution you want if your printer supports this feature.

- **Printer Color Profile:** Gives the current color profile.

- **Print to File:** Creates a file that can be printed from DOS or from some other computer that does not have the Corel program.

- **For Mac:** If you have a PostScript printer, you can opt to print to a file that a Macintosh computer can read and print.

- **Collate Copies:** Check this option if you want your documents collated.

- **Copies:** You can print as many as 999 copies of the drawing.

Clicking on the Print Options button in the Print dialog box opens the following additional dialog box:

Print...

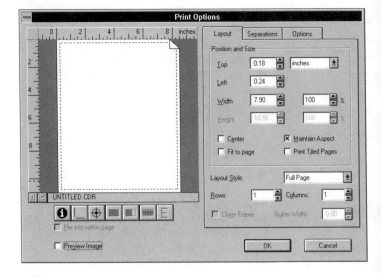

Reference tab options:

The row of icons directly below the preview window allows you to add standard printer's marks to a drawing. They are, from left to right:

- **ⓘ** Prints filename, current date and time, tile, and plate number on every printable page. Also includes other stuff, such as color profile, color name, and screen frequency on color separations.
- **⌐** Prints crop marks.
- **⊕** Prints registration marks.
- **▥** Prints a calibration bar (RGBCYM).
- **▥** Prints densitometer scale on each page.
- **▥** Creates reversed image of drawing to image directly on film.
- **E** Select this option if your printer or service bureau wants film printed emulsion side down.

Layout tab options:

✔ The Position and Size section allows you to adjust the drawing's size and position on the page. Selecting the Maintain Aspect box resizes the drawing proportionally when previewed and printed. Print Tile Pages prints parts of the drawing that extend beyond the printable page on separate pages (useful for posters and signs).

Print... 85

- If you're proofing really small stuff, you can use Fit to Page to blow the critter up so that you can see it more easily.

- The Layout Style drop-down list lets you select from any of the predefined styles. See Page Setup for more information.

- Enter values in the Rows, Columns, and Gutter Width boxes to divide the printed page into segments, and check the Clone Frame box if you want to copy the contents of one segment to all the others.

Separations tab options:

- Checking the Print Separations box prints the colors (usually CMYK and any spot colors) in halftone separations. Click on any colors that you want to separate in the Colors area.

- The In Color checkbox, when checked, prints the separations in color. This option is available only if you are printing to a file or to a color printer.

- Leave the Use Custom Halftone box unchecked unless you are really advanced at determining halftone screen angles and frequencies. The same goes for the Edit button, with which you make custom modifications to those angles and frequencies.

- Auto Trapping adds traps to certain objects.

- If you're really advanced at trapping, spreading, and choking, you probably should use Overprint instead of Auto Trapping. See Overprint Line and Overprint Fill.

Options tab options:

- **Screen Frequency:** Determines the halftone screen frequency used to print the drawing.

- **Set Flatness To:** Determines how many segments PostScript printers use to draw a curve. If you are getting limit-check errors, increase this number to simplify the drawing.

- **Auto Increase Flatness:** When checked, automatically increases the flatness setting until the drawing is simple enough to print.

- **Fountain Steps:** Tells CorelDraw how many stripes or bands to use to make a fountain fill.

- **Download Type 1 Fonts:** Places the fonts used in the drawing in the print file.

- **Convert TrueType to Type 1:** Converts all TrueType fonts to Type 1, making the file smaller.

Print Merge...

More stuff

Many of the commands in the Print Options dialog boxes are very advanced, and unless you really need to make some modifications, the defaults work pretty well.

Select the Preview Image box for a print preview, but don't be overly concerned if your preview area remains blank. I think Corel's programmers went to lunch when this bit of code was being developed. Everything still prints OK, though.

For more information about printing, see Chapter 13 in *CorelDRAW! 5 For Dummies*.

Print Merge...

This command is simply boss for creating certificates and similar individualized doodads. You first need to prepare an ASCII Merge file by following some rather stringent rules; see "Preparing the Merge File" in Volume One of the CorelDraw manual or, better yet, refer to *CorelDRAW! 5 For Dummies*.

Using Print Merge

1. Open the drawing you want to use as the template.
2. From the File menu, choose Print Merge, which opens a directory-style dialog box.
3. Select the prepared text file.
4. Click on OK. The Print Options dialog box opens.
5. Select the print options you want.
6. Click on OK.

More stuff

You can merge only Artistic text objects, and you should not attempt to merge text that has been blended, extruded, fitted to a path, or had differing attributes applied to individual characters.

Print Setup...

Selects the printer that will print the drawing.

Using Print Setup

1. Choose Print Setup from the File menu.

2. Select a printer from the list of installed printers.
3. Select the Print Quality if the selected printer has the capability to print at different resolutions.
4. Click on the Setup button to open the Windows printer setup dialog box specific to the selected printer.

More stuff

See *Windows 3.1 For Dummies,* Second Edition for an explanation of the Control Panel⇨Printers dialog box.

Redo

When you change your mind and want to put something back the way it was before you selected the Undo command, Redo is for you.

Digital rodent replacement

Alt+Enter

Using Redo

Choose Redo from the Edit menu. Tough.

More stuff

The Redo command becomes available only after you issue an Undo command. The wording of the command in the menu changes, depending on the last command that was undone.

Refresh Window

CorelDraw has a tendency to leave little bug tracks behind every now and again. The Refresh Window command forces a redraw of the screen and makes CorelDraw clean up after itself.

Digital rodent replacement

Ctrl+W

Using Refresh Window

Choose Refresh Window from the View menu.

88 Repeat

More stuff

You can also refresh the window by clicking on the thumb (that little square slider thing) in the horizontal or vertical scroll bar.

Repeat

If possible, the Repeat command reperforms the last command that was issued. It can be quite useful if you have several objects that need to be rotated, stretched, or whatever in the same way.

Digital rodent replacement

Ctrl+R

Using Repeat

Choose Repeat from the Edit menu.

More stuff

The wording of the command in the menu changes depending on the last command that was undone.

Replace...

Your typical, everyday, text-replacing doodad. Lets you find and replace text in a document.

Using Replace

1. Choose Replace from the Text menu. You see this dialog box.

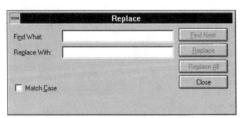

2. Enter the text to search for in the Find What: box.
3. Enter the new text in the Replace With: box.

Revert To Master

4. If you want to search only for exact case matches, select the Match Case checkbox.

5. Click on the Replace button to find the next instance of the text and then Replace again to go on searching, *or*

   Click on the Replace All button to automatically replace every instance of the text in the document.

6. To exit, click on the Close button.

More stuff

The Find command searches from the insertion point to the end of the document. When you reach the end, a dialog box appears asking whether you want to continue searching from the beginning.

Be careful when clicking on Replace All. If you just put in the letters you want to replace, like *pot,* CorelDraw merrily replaces every instance of those three letters, no matter where they are. *Pot, pot*ato(e), or s*pot*: Draw does not differentiate. (Hint: When you're constructing your replace string, don't forget that you can include spaces but not wildcards.)

Revert To Master

Restores the Master's outline, fill, shape, and effects to a selected clone.

Using Revert To Master

1. Select the clone you want to revert.

2. Open the Object Menu by clicking on the clone with the right mouse button.

3. Choose Revert To Master from the Object Menu. The Revert To Master dialog box opens.

4. Select the stuff that you want to restore. The selection boxes are grayed out for things that have not been modified on the clone.

Revert to Style

More stuff

If you defined a function for the right mouse button (see Preferences), you have to click the right button and hold it down for a second or so to make the Object Menu appear.

 This command works only on objects that you have cloned by using the Clone command in the Edit menu. It does not work on effects that you have cloned by using the Clone command in the Effects menu.

The Object Menu has a way of staying around long after you're done with it on some systems. If this problem occurs, save your work immediately, close the program, and restart.

Revert To Style

Selecting this command from the Object Menu reapplies the attributes that were defined for the object when you first applied a style to it or saved it as a style.

 See Apply Style for information about styles.

Using Revert To Style

1. Select the object you want to revert.
2. Open the Object Menu by clicking on it with the right mouse button.
3. Choose Revert To Style.

More stuff

 If you defined a function for the right mouse button (see Preferences), you have to depress the right button and hold it down for a second or so to make the Object Menu appear.

The Object Menu has a way of staying around long after you're done with it on some systems. If this problem occurs, save your work immediately. Then close the program and restart it.

Roll-Ups...

Allows you to open and arrange roll-ups and set which ones display on startup.

Using Roll-Ups

1. Choose Roll-Ups from the View menu.
2. Make any modifications you want in the dialog box.

- **Roll-ups:** Lists all the roll-ups in CorelDraw. All active ones are noted with an icon to their left in the scrolling listbox.

- **Visible:** Makes all roll-ups you select (Ctrl+click to select noncontiguous items in a list) in the roll-ups list visible.

- **Arranged:** Lines up the visible roll-ups in a pleasing manner.

- **Rolled Down:** Displays the roll-ups with their drawers down.

- **Select All:** Makes all the roll-ups displayed in the roll-ups list visible, and you thereby risk losing all your work.

- **Deselect All:** Returns all roll-ups to invisibility.

- **Start Up Setting:** Selects the startup roll-ups of your choice. Selecting several and then choosing Custom from the Start Up Setting list enables the Custom button. This lets you name a startup preference.

3. Click on OK.

More stuff

Each cute little roll-up eats up some of your precious Windows resources. Unfortunately, when a sufficient number of those resources are used up, your system just might freeze, requiring a warm or cold boot to get it going again. This means that everything you did since the last save is history.

Rulers

Rulers

Toggles the display of the rulers on and off.

Using Rulers

Choose Rulers from the View menu. If the command is checked, the rulers are visible; choose the command again to turn them off.

More stuff

 To change the unit of measurement on the rulers, choose the units for the Horizontal and Vertical Grid Frequency drop-down lists from the Grid & Scale Setup dialog box found under the Layout menu.

Save, Save As...

Saves a document to disk. When you save a document for the first time, the Save As dialog box opens to let you name the document. Any subsequent save uses the same name, and the dialog box does not open. You can also use the Save As command to save an existing file in a different name, location, or format or to add keywords and notes to an existing drawing.

Digital rodent replacement

Ctrl+S

Ribbon bar icon

Using Save & Save As

1. Choose Save (or Save As) from the File menu.

2. If you choose the Save command and the drawing already has a name, the drawing is saved to disk.

3. If this is the first time the drawing has been saved or if you choose the Save As command, the Save Drawing dialog box opens.

4. Give the file a name and select the drive and directory where it is to be stored.

5. If you want to save it in another CorelDraw format (for Version 3 or 4), select that format from the Version drop-down list.

Save As Style... (Object Menu)

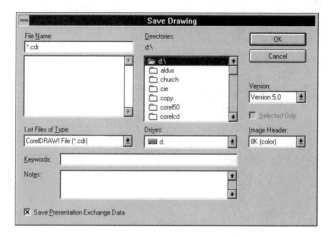

6. Enter keywords, separated by commas, in the Keywords area and enter any notes you want to attach to the drawing in the Notes area.
7. Click on OK.

More stuff

The keywords you enter in the Keywords box allow you to do a search for the keywords when you open or view your drawing at a later date.

The checkbox titled Save Presentation Exchange Data should be left checked unless you really know what you're doing. Presentation exchange data is the information used to send the object to an output device, such as a printer or your monitor.

Save As Style... (Object Menu)

Available from the Object Menu, this command allows you to save attributes and effects, such as font information, fills, and perspective, as a style that you can apply to other objects by using the Apply Style command.

See Apply Style for information about attaching saved styles to objects.

Digital rodent replacement

Click the right mouse button on the selected object to open the Object Menu.

Screen/Menu Help...

Using Save As Style

After you have modified an object, you can save those modifications as a style by following these steps:

1. Select the object or text you want to change.
2. Choose Save As Style from the Object Menu (right mouse button).
3. Select the attributes and effects that you want to include in the style from the dialog box that opens.
4. Give the style a Name.
5. Click on OK.

More stuff

The three different types of styles are Artistic text, Paragraph text, and Graphic. The styles for Artistic and Paragraph text include Fills, Outlines, Font Style, and Size, while Graphic styles include Special Effects (envelopes, extrudes, and so on) as well as Outlines and Fills. The selections in the Include dialog box vary according to the type of object you selected and the modifications that you have made to it.

Styles that have been defined through the Object Menu also appear in the Styles roll-up (Ctrl+F5).

Screen/Menu Help...

Accesses CorelDraw's interactive help.

Digital rodent replacement

Shift+F1

Using Screen/Menu Help

1. Choose Screen/Menu Help from the Help menu. The cursor changes to a question mark.
2. From a menu, select the item or function about which you want help or click on it on the desktop. A matching help topic opens.

Search For Help On...

Opens up a list of help topics.

Digital rodent replacement
Ctrl+F1

Using Search For Help On

1. Choose Search For Help On from the Help menu.
2. In the Search dialog box, type the name of the command you want help on or select it from the list.
3. Click on the Show Topics button.
4. Select a topic from the lower listbox and click on the Go To button.

Select All

Selects all objects in the drawing, even those that do not appear in the current view.

Using Select All

Choose Select All from the Edit menu.

More stuff

This command is useful in locating objects that have gotten lost when being imported or that have wandered off the viewing area. Use Select All and then choose the Zoom To Selected tool from the Zoom flyout menu. If the object is there, you should see it.

Select Clones

Selects all the objects that have been cloned from the master. You can then manipulate the little clonelets or find out where they're hiding.

Using Select Clones

1. Select the Master object.
2. Open the Object Menu by clicking on the selected Master object with the right mouse button.
3. Choose the Select Clones command.

More stuff

If you defined a function for the right mouse button, you have to click and hold down the right button for a second or two to open the Object Menu.

Select Master

Selects the Master object that derives the selected clone. This command is identical to Select Clone. The Select command in the Object Menu reads either Master or Clone, depending on which type of object you select before you open the Object Menu.

Separations, Color

See Print, Separations tab.

Separate

Using this command is the best way to tear asunder unwanted blends, contours, extrudes, clones, and fitted text. The original objects are separated from the intermediate steps, and each is maintained as a separate object.

Using Separate

Select the blended, contoured, extruded, cloned, or text-fitted object that you want to separate. Then choose Separate from the Arrange menu.

Snap To Grid   97

More stuff

You can create some really interesting effects by using, for example, just the extrusion without the original extruded object.

Show Grid

Makes the grid visible on-screen.

Using Show Grid

To make the grid visible, choose Grid & Scale Setup from the Layout menu. Then activate the Show Grid checkbox in the resulting dialog box.

More stuff

For more information about Grids, see Grid & Scale Setup.

Snap To Grid

Toggles Snap To Grid on and off. When active (checked), the cursor, as well as the side of any object, is forced to conform to the grid points set up in the Grid & Scale Setup dialog box. It makes grids "sticky" and attractive.

Digital rodent replacement

Ctrl+Y

Using Snap To Grid

To make the grid sticky, choose Snap To Grid from the Layout menu.

More stuff

For more information about Grids, see Grid & Scale Setup.

When active, text snaps to the grid by using the baseline for vertical movements. The justification option in the Character or Edit Text dialog boxes determines the snap point for horizontal text movement.

The Snap To pecking order is as follows: Snap To Objects always takes priority over Snap To Grid and Snap To Guidelines. Snap To Guidelines takes priority over Snap To Grid.

Snap To Guidelines

Toggles Snap To Guidelines on and off. When active (checked), the cursor, as well as the sides of all objects, is attracted to guidelines dragged into the drawing from the rulers or set up in the Guidelines Setup dialog box.

Ribbon bar icon

Using Snap To Guidelines

To make the guidelines sticky, choose Snap To Guidelines from the Layout menu.

More stuff

For more information about Guidelines, see Guidelines Setup.

The Snap To pecking order is as follows: Snap To Objects always takes priority over Snap To Grid and Snap To Guidelines. Snap To Guidelines takes priority over Snap To Grid.

Snap To Objects

Toggles Snap To Objects on and off. When active (checked), any moving object snaps to a snap point on a stationary object. The snap points vary with the type of object but usually are the same as the node handles you see when you select the object with the Arrow tool.

Using Snap To Objects

To toggle Snap To Objects on and off, choose Snap To Objects from the Layout menu.

More stuff

The Snap To pecking order is: Snap To Objects always takes priority over Snap To Grid and Snap To Guidelines. Snap To Guidelines takes priority over Snap To Grid.

Spell Checker...

Checks your spellin'.

Straighten Text 99

Using Spell Checker

1. Select the Artistic or Paragraph text that you want to check.
2. Choose Spell Checker from the Text menu to open the Spell Check dialog box.

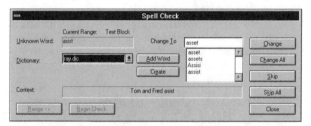

3. Click on the Begin Check button.
4. CorelDraw displays misspelled words in the Unknown Word box, and the words surrounding the misspelled words appear in the Context area.
5. Select an alternative word from the scrolling list or type the correction in the Change To box.
6. Repeat Steps 3 through 5 until the `Spell check finished` message appears.

More stuff

You can create a custom dictionary by clicking on the Create button and then entering a name in the resulting dialog box. To use this custom dictionary, you must then select it from the Dictionary drop-down list in the Spell Check dialog box. After you have defined and selected a dictionary, you then can add your own or new words to it by clicking on the Add Word button when you know that the spelling is correct.

If the Add Word button is grayed out, you either have not created a custom dictionary or have not selected one from the Dictionary drop-down list.

See TypeAssist for help in automatically correcting spelling and common typos.

Straighten Text

Restores all text in the selected object to the baseline and resets the vertical and angle shifts to zero. Makes your letters walk the straight, if not the narrow.

Using Straighten Text

Select the text objects that you want to straighten and then choose Straighten Text from the Text menu.

More stuff

If you want to use the Straighten Text command on grouped objects, use the Separate command in the Arrange menu first. The Straighten Text command does not affect text-spacing options that you set with the Edit Text or Paragraph commands.

Styles Roll-Up

Applies styles and manages style templates. You can apply styles created from the Object Menu, delete styles from a template, or load different templates of style collections that you have created. Supermodels have nothing on this command (except beauty and lots of bucks, that is).

Digital rodent replacement

Ctrl+F5

Using the Styles roll-up

To apply a predefined style:

1. Select the object to which you want to apply the style.
2. Choose Styles Roll-Up from the Layout menu.
3. In the Styles roll-up, select the style that you want to apply from the list. To see the available styles for Artistic text, Paragraph text, or Graphic, click on the appropriate button in the roll-up.

4. Click on Apply.

Symbols Roll-Up 101

To manage existing styles:

1. Choose Styles Roll-Up from the Layout menu.
2. Click on the small triangle in the upper portion of the roll-up to open a style-managing flyout doohickey.

3. From here, you can select from the following:

   - **Load Styles...** opens a dialog box that lets you load a different style template.

   - **Save Template...** opens a dialog box that lets you save the current styles as a new or modified template.

   - **Set Hotkeys...** opens a dialog box that allows you to assign key combination shortcuts to your styles.

   - **Delete Style** gets rid of your mistakes.

   - **Find** finds objects that have a selected style.

To create a style, see Save As Style.

More stuff

The three different types of styles are Artistic text, Paragraph text, and Graphic. The styles for Artistic and Paragraph text include Fills, Outlines, Font Style, and Size; while Graphic styles include Special Effects (envelopes, extrudes, and so on), Outlines, and Fills.

If you use certain styles over and over again, you should assign hot key combinations to them. Choose Set Hotkeys from the flyout menu to do so.

Symbols Roll-Up

Opens up a display of hundreds of symbols that you can use as part of your drawings.

Symbols Roll-Up

Digital rodent replacement
Ctrl+F11

Ribbon bar icon

Using the Symbols roll-up

1. Choose Symbols Roll-Up from the Special menu. The roll-up appears.

2. Select a symbol library from the drop-down list.

3. Enter the symbol number in the # box or drag the symbol you want into the work area.

4. If you want the symbol displayed in a tile pattern, select the Tile box.

5. If you want the symbol in a particular size, include that size in the Size box. (Anything from .01 to 30 inches is okay.)

6. The Options button allows you to adjust the grid size for tiled symbols, and selecting the Proportional Sizing box maintains the aspect ratio of the symbol when a corner handle is dragged.

More stuff

You can break apart the symbols and recombine them any way you want.

For more information about the Symbols roll-up, see Chapter 10 in *CorelDRAW! 5 For Dummies*.

Text Roll-Up

All the handy text manipulation tools are in one place. Adjust character, paragraph, and frame attributes without messing around with a multitude of other menus.

Digital rodent replacement
Ctrl+F2

Using the Text roll-up

1. Choose Text Roll-Up from the Text menu.
2. Select the desired font, attributes, size, and alignment from the roll-up.

3. To change character-specific settings, click on the Character Attributes button.

   See Character for a discussion of the stuff that you can modify here.

4. To change paragraph-specific settings, click on the Paragraph button.

   See Paragraph for a discussion of the stuff that you can modify here.

5. To change frame-specific settings, click on the Frame button.

   See Frame for a discussion of the stuff that you can modify here.

   The initial release of CorelDraw 5 refuses to do the width and gutter calculations for you. If you really must use this command, you need to do the subtraction yourself. Because the measurements entered here override the measurements entered in page setup, you can easily make the frame so wide that it does not all print.

6. To apply changes to all linked frames in a story, click on the Apply to All Frames button.

7. To apply changes to the current frame, as well as to all linked frames that are after the current one, click on the Apply to Rest of Frames button.

8. Click on Apply when you have selected all the Text options.

More stuff

Commands that apply to linked frames are available only for Paragraph text.

Thesaurus...

Look up synonyms and other fun words to use in your drawings.

Using Thesaurus

1. Select the word for which you want a synonym.

2. Choose Thesaurus from the Text menu to access the Thesaurus dialog box.

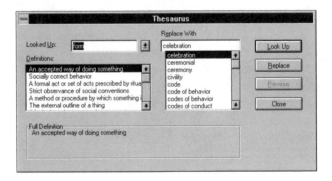

3. If the word has multiple meanings, select the meaning you want from the Definitions list.

4. Select the desired substitute from the Replace With: list.

5. Click on the Replace button.

Toolbox 105

More stuff

You can look up words directly in the Thesaurus by typing the word you want to change in the Looked Up box and clicking on the Look Up button.

For more information about the Thesaurus, see Chapter 10 in *CorelDRAW! 5 For Dummies*.

Toolbox

- ➪ Visible
- ➪ Floating

Lets you see the toolbox, or not see the toolbox, in two attractive versions and in the location of your choice.

Using Toolbox

To hide or show the toolbox, choose Visible from the Toolbox flyout in the View menu.

If you want the toolbox to float so that you can reposition it wherever you want, choose Floating from the Toolbox flyout in the View menu.

More stuff

If you want to see all of CorelDraw's tools, you can display them all by selecting Grouped from the Control menu of the toolbox after it has been made floating. In other words, do this:

1. Choose Floating from the Toolbox flyout in the View menu.
2. Choose Grouped from the Control menu of the floating toolbox. (The Control menu is the one that looks like a spacebar or a dash in the upper-left corner of the box.)

Transform Roll-Up

Positions graphics and other stuff very precisely. Adjusts the placement, size, scale, angle of rotation, and skew of a selected object. This command is best used by people who really want to be horribly accurate or who need to repeat identical measurements over and over and have little use for that mouse, anyway.

Digital rodent replacement
Alt+F7

Using the Transform roll-up

The five buttons that run along the top of the roll-up control the various functions of the command. They are Place, Rotate, Scale and Mirror, Size, and Skew.

To oh-so-precisely place an object in a drawing or move it about exactly so much, follow these steps:

1. Select the object that you want to place or move.
2. Choose Transform Roll-Up from the Effects menu.
3. Click on the Place button (the first button icon at the top of the roll-up) to open the placement commands.

4. Click on the triangle located next to the Relative Position box to open an anchor node display. The displayed squares represent the sizing handles and the center point of the selected object. The node that you select determines the spot from which the measurement is taken.
5. Choose the node that you want to serve as the anchor.
6. If you want to move the object horizontally or vertically by a specific amount, check the Relative Position box.

Transform Roll-Up 107

7. Enter measurements in the H (horizontal) and V (vertical) boxes. If the Relative Position box is checked, enter the amount of movement you want from the current position. If the Relative Position box is not checked, enter the measurements from the ruler where you want the anchor node to be placed.

8. Click on Apply to apply the placement to the object, or click on Apply To Duplicate to create a new object at the specified position.

To oh-so-precisely rotate an object in a drawing, follow these steps:

1. Select the object that you want to rotate.
2. Choose Transform Roll-Up from the Effects menu.
3. Click on the Rotate button (the second button) to open the rotation commands.

4. Click on the triangle located next to the Relative Position box to open a display of anchor nodes. The node that you select becomes the center of rotation.
5. Choose the node that you want to serve as the anchor.
6. Enter the angle of rotation that you want in the Angle of Rotation box (positive numbers rotate the object counter-clockwise; negative numbers rotate it clockwise).

If you don't want to use any of the handles or the center of the object as the center of rotation, you can check the Relative Center box and enter measurements in the H and V boxes to define a specific center of rotation. All this stuff is much easier with the mouse. Double-click on the object until the rotation arrows appear and then drag the little bulls-eye doodad (the center of rotation) to the point about which you want the object to rotate.

Transform Roll-Up

7. Click on Apply to apply the rotation to the object, or click on Apply To Duplicate to create a new object with the specified rotation.

To oh-so-precisely scale an object in a drawing, follow these steps:

1. Select the object that you want to scale.
2. Choose Transform Roll-Up from the Effects menu.
3. Click on the Scale button (the third button) to open the scale commands.

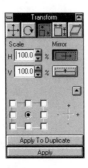

4. Enter the percentages of scale that you want in the H and V boxes. To maintain the object's aspect, enter identical measurements in the H and V boxes. To stretch the object, enter a larger or smaller number in one or the other.

All this stuff is bunches easier with the mouse, if somewhat less precise. Click on the object until the selection handles appear and then drag the corner handles to scale the object proportionally or the side handles to stretch it disproportionally.

5. If you want to mirror the object, press the horizontal or vertical mirror button, or both.
6. Click on Apply to apply the scale to the object, or click on Apply To Duplicate to create a new object of the specified size.

To precisely size an object, follow these steps:

1. Select the object that you want to size.
2. Choose Transform Roll-Up from the Effects menu.
3. Click on the Size button (the fourth button) to open the scale commands.

Transform Roll-Up 109

4. Enter the new measurements in the H and V boxes.

Yep, you can do this with the mouse. Click on the object until the selection handles appear and then drag the corner handles to scale the object or the side handles to stretch it. Check out the status line while you're dragging or scaling. The percentage of change appears, giving you a pretty good guidepost.

5. Click on Apply to apply the size to the object, or click on Apply To Duplicate to create a new object with the specified size.

To precisely skew an object, follow these steps:

1. Select the object that you want to squish.
2. Choose Transform Roll-Up from the Effects menu.
3. Click on the Skew button (the last button) to open the skew commands.

4. Enter the amount of skew that you want in the H and V boxes.

Yep, you can do this with the mouse, too. Double-click on the object until the rotation arrows appear and then drag one of the four side handles to skew the object. Check out the status line while you're skewing. The skew angle appears, giving you a pretty good idea of just how warped your object is getting.

5. Click on Apply to apply the skew to the object, or click on Apply To Duplicate to create a new object with the specified skew.

More stuff

The unit of measure used in the Transform roll-up is selected in the Page Distance section of the Grid & Scale Setup dialog box. See the Grid & Scale Setup command if you want to change the measurement system.

Trim

More fun than making paper dolls. When used on overlapping objects, the Trim command cuts out the overlapping area from the last object selected to make it conform to the outline of the first object. You have to move the objects apart to see the effect of the trim.

Using Trim

Select the two overlapping objects that you want to trim and then choose Trim from the Arrange menu.

More stuff

If you marquee-select the two objects, the last one created — or the object in the highest arrangement order — is the one that is trimmed. This command is really neat for leaving holes in objects, such as part of a star or a shape on an animal.

Tutorial

This command is a wonderful way to while away an hour or two and learn more about some neat feature of CorelDraw. It's fun and entertaining, and your boss may find it hard to yell at you because it's educational, too.

Using Tutorial

Choose Tutorial from the Help menu to open the Learning CorelDRAW dialog box. Then click on the button that represents the topic you want to learn about.

Type Assist... 111

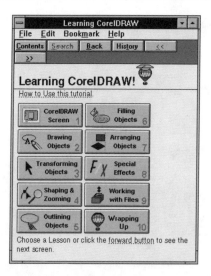

Type Assist...

 You're usually better off to use programs that have been specifically designed for the task that you want to accomplish. Use a word processor for word processing, a draw program for drawing, and so on.

That hint aside, Type Assist automatically corrects some common keyboarding errors for you.

Using Type Assist

1. Choose Type Assist from the Text menu.
2. Choose the stuff that you want CorelDraw to fix in the Type Assist dialog box:
   - Capitalize First Letter of Sentence
   - Change Straight Quotes to Typographic Quotes
   - Correct Two Initial Capitals
   - Capitalize Names of Days
   - Replace Text While Typing
3. Click on OK.

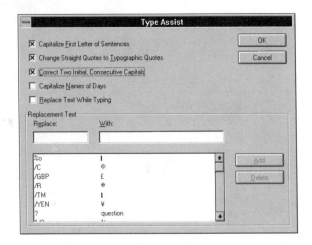

More stuff

Although it is best to do your typing in a word processor, sometimes it's easier to do it in CorelDraw. If you simply aren't into proofreading, these commands may be of some use. One neat feature is the automatic replacement of a text string with another. For instance, automatically replacing /R with the registered mark can save you quite a bit of time in looking through various symbol sets. You can design your own replacements and add them to the Replacement Text boxes by clicking on the Add button.

Undo

Reverses the last action(s) that you performed in the current session. The Undo command name reflects the command name of your last action.

Digital rodent replacement

Ctrl+Z

Using Undo

Choose Undo from the Edit menu.

More stuff

You can set the number of levels of undo (from 1 to 99) in the General tab of the Preferences dialog box (Ctrl+J). The more

Update Style... (Object Menu)

levels of undo you choose, the more computer memory is required. You cannot undo the following actions:

- Change of view (Zoom and so on)
- File operations (Open, Save, and so on)
- Selection operations

Update Style... (Object Menu)

Changes an existing style. Use this command to modify the attributes of an existing style or to save changes to an existing style with a new name.

Using Update Style

After you have modified an object's style, you save those modifications as either a new style or as a change to the existing style by following these steps:

1. Hold down the right mouse button while pointing to the object whose style you want to modify. Doing so opens the Object Menu.
2. Choose Update Style from the Object Menu.
3. Select the attributes and effects that you want to include in the style from the Update Style dialog box.

Ungroup

4. Give the style a name in the <u>N</u>ame box if you're creating a new style.
5. Click on OK.

More stuff

The three different types of styles are Artistic text, Paragraph text, and Graphic. The styles for Artistic and Paragraph text include Fills, Outlines, Font style, and Size; while Graphic styles include Special effects (envelopes, extrudes, and so on), Outlines, and Fills. The selections in the Include dialog box vary according to the type of object you select and the modifications that you make to it.

Styles that you have defined or updated through the Object Menu also appear in the Styles roll-up (Ctrl+F5).

<u>U</u>ngroup

Ungroups the groups that you have put together by using the <u>G</u>roup command.

Digital rodent replacement

Ctrl+U

Using <u>U</u>ngroup

Select the group that you want to ungroup and then choose <u>U</u>ngroup from the <u>A</u>rrange menu.

More stuff

You can often use <u>U</u>ngroup on imported graphics, like WMF files, to change them or delete unwanted areas and objects from them.

If you have nested groups within groups, using the <u>U</u>ngroup command breaks apart one group at a time.

<u>W</u>eld

Every bit as much fun as <u>T</u>rim. When used on overlapping objects, the <u>W</u>eld command cements the two objects together. The resulting curve object assumes the fill and attributes of the last selected of the two overlapping objects.

Using Weld

Select the two overlapping objects that you want to weld. Then choose Weld from the Arrange menu.

More stuff

If you select the two objects with a marquee, the new curve object assumes the fill and other attributes of the last one you created.

Wireframe

Toggles between the full-blown drawing in full view and a much-quicker-to-display-on-screen outline only view.

Digital rodent replacement

Shift+F9

Ribbon bar icon

Using Wireframe

To toggle between Wireframe and Show Fill preview modes, choose Wireframe from the View menu.

More stuff

If you are in Wireframe view and want to select an object, you must click on the outline. Clicking in the center of the object does not work like it does in Show Fill view.

The Part of Tools and Other Neato Stuff

CorelDraw has nine major tools: Pick, Shape, Zoom, Pencil, Rectangle, Ellipse, Text, Outline Pen, and Fill. Several of these tools have variants, so all in all you can do 48 different things right from the Tools menu. That's a bunch of stuff. The tools are listed here in their order of appearance on-screen.

You may want to pay particular attention to the shortcuts that are available for selecting the various tools and make one or two of them a permanent part of your Corelius Drawius modus operandi.

Pick Tool

 You use the Pick tool to pick, or select, objects or groups of objects. You can also use it to stretch, scale, rotate, and skew objects after you select them.

Shortcuts

Press the spacebar while using any tool (other than Text tools) to select the Pick tool. Press Ctrl+spacebar while using Text tools to select the Pick tool.

Press the spacebar while the Pick tool is selected to use the last tool that was active.

Double-click on the Pick tool to select all objects in the drawing.

Using the Pick tool

To select an object, point to it with the Pick tool and click. If the object is filled, you can point anywhere on the object. If the object has no fill or if you are in Wireframe view, you have to click on the outline.

To select multiple objects, you can hold down the Shift key while you click on each object in succession, or you can drag a marquee box around the objects you want to select. (To drag a marquee box, point outside the objects, click the left mouse button, and drag a box that surrounds all the objects that you want to select.)

 If the MultiLayer option is turned on in the Layers roll-up, you can select objects that are placed on different layers. If it isn't turned on, you can't.

Status line information

When you select a single object, the status line tells you what type of object it is (text, rectangle, ellipse, bitmap, or whatever), which layer the object is on, and what its Outline and Fill attributes are. When you have selected more than one object, the status line displays the number of objects you selected.

Shape Tool

 The function of the Shape tool varies with the type of object that is selected. In general, the Shape tool is used to modify the shape of a portion of an object.

Shortcut

To select the Shape tool without using the mouse, press F10.

Using the Shape tool

- **Lines and curves:** Use the Shape tool to move any node or control point. Also, double-clicking on a node opens the Node Edit roll-up.

- **Text:** Selecting Paragraph or Artistic text with the Shape tool allows you to adjust spacing and positioning of characters. Dragging the large arrowheads that appear near the bottom of the text block adjusts the space between letters and the space between lines (*tracking* and *leading*, respectively).

    You can adjust the space between individual letters (*kerning*) by dragging the small box along the baseline of the letter to a new horizontal or vertical position.

- **Bitmaps:** Use the Shape tool to crop bitmaps by dragging the selection handles to show just the portion of the image that you want.

- **Rectangles and squares:** Use the Shape tool to round the corners of these shapes. Drag a corner handle along the side of the shape.

- **Ellipses and circles:** Use the Shape tool to create arcs and wedges by dragging the control point around the curve.

Status line information

The status line displays axis and distance information when the Shape tool is used on a line or a curve, intercharacter and interline information when used on text, percentage cropping information when used on bitmaps, corner radius information when used on squares and rectangles, and angle information when used on circles and ellipses.

Zoom Tools

You can use these six different tools to view all, or parts, of a drawing.

Pencil Tools

Tool	Name	What It Does
🔍	Zoom In tool	Magnifies a part of the screen. To get a close-up view of a portion of your drawing, drag a marquee box around the area that you want to see by using the Zoom In tool.
🔍	Zoom Out tool	Zooms out by a factor of two each time you click anywhere on the drawing. The first click returns you to the view you were using before your last zoom-in.
1·1	Actual Size tool	Click on this icon to display the drawing at the same size that it will print (if you have a 14- to 15-inch monitor).
	Zoom to Selected tool	Zooms in or out to show all selected objects.
	Fit in Window tool	Zooms to bring all objects in the drawing into view.
	Show Page tool	Zooms to display the printable page.

Shortcuts

Press F2 to select the Zoom In tool.

Press F3 to return to the preceding view or to zoom out by a factor of two.

Press F4 to bring all objects in a drawing into view.

Pencil Tools

Use these tools to draw lines, curves, and dimension lines. Keeping the mouse button depressed on the Pencil tool opens a menu that lets you choose from six other drawing tools.

Ellipse Tool

Tool	Name	What It Does
	Freehand tool	Use like you would a pen on paper, just a lot more awkwardly.
	Bezier tool	Offers connect-the-dots drawing with the added feature of control points.
	Dimension lines	You see dimension lines on blueprints and the like. They are lines with a notation of the distance that the line represents in the middle of them. You can mess with the font and measurement style in the Dimension Lines roll-up by pressing Alt+F2.
	Callout tool	Draws those arrow-pointing-to-it-that-comes-from-an-explanation-of-what-it-is things.

Rectangle Tool

  Use this tool to draw rectangles and squares.

Shortcuts

Pressing F6 selects the Rectangle tool.

To create a page frame, double-click on the Rectangle tool.

To immediately select a rectangle after creating it with the Rectangle tool, press the spacebar.

To toggle between the Pick tool and the Rectangle tool you just used, press the spacebar.

Status line information

The status line displays the dimensions of the object as you create it.

Ellipse Tool

  Use this tool to draw ellipses and circles.

Text Tool

Shortcuts

Pressing F7 selects the Ellipse tool.

To immediately select an ellipse after creating it with the Ellipse tool, press the spacebar.

To toggle between the Ellipse tool and the Rectangle tool you just used, press the spacebar.

Status line information

The status line displays the dimensions of the object as you create it.

Text Tool

Add Artistic text, Paragraph text, and symbols to a drawing with these tools.

Shortcuts

Press F8 to select the Artistic Text tool.

Press Shift+F8 to select the Paragraph Text tool.

Double-click on the Text tool to open the Text roll-up.

Using the Text tools

 Click in the drawing window where you want to place the Artistic text.

 Drag a frame in the drawing where you want to place the Paragraph text.

Outline Pen Tools

Choose outline thickness and color with these tools.

Fill Tools   121

Tool	What It Does
	Opens the Outline Pen dialog box, which allows you to set line thickness and pattern, pen effects, and arrowheads.
	Opens the Pen roll-up. You can do the same stuff in the roll-up that you can do in the Outline Pen dialog box, but the roll-up hangs around for future use.
	You can select from preset line widths here. The selections are none, .2, 2, 8, 16, and 24 points.
	Opens the Outline Color dialog box, which allows you to choose a custom outline color.
	Lets you choose from a preselected series of black, white, and gray outline colors. The selections are white, black, and grays of 10, 30, 50, 70, and 90 percent.

Shortcuts

Press F12 with an object selected to open the Outline Pen dialog box.

Press Shift+F12 with an object selected to open the Outline Color dialog box.

Fill Tools

Use these tools to set an object's fill.

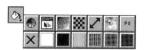

Tool	What It Does
	Opens the Uniform Fill dialog box to select or create a uniform color fill.
	Opens the Fill roll-up for handy access to various fills.
	Opens the Fountain Fill dialog box.
	Opens the Two-Color Pattern dialog box.

(continued)

Fill Tools

Tool	What It Does
	Opens the Load Full Color Pattern dialog box so that you can choose a pattern to use as the fill.
	Opens the Texture Fills dialog box.
	If your printer can handle it, clicking on this icon opens the PostScript Textures Fills dialog box. Refer to Volume One, Appendix D of the CorelDRAW! 5 manual for pictures of each PostScript fill.
	Removes fill from an object, leaving it transparent.
	Lets you choose from a preselected series of black, white, and gray fills. The selections are white, black, and grays of 10, 30, 50, 70, and 90 percent.

Shortcuts

Use the on-screen palette to fill objects with uniform colors.

Press Shift+F11 to open the Uniform Fill dialog box.

Part II

The Dummies Guide to CorelPhoto-Paint

CorelPhoto-Paint is an extremely complex program that is not at all well documented. In the pages that I have to discuss the program, I can't do much more than tell you what the commands are and what they do. If you need in-depth knowledge of Photo-Paint, the best suggestion I can make is to get *CorelDRAW! 5 For Dummies,* open to Chapters 14 and 15, and play with the program. Use this quick reference to find out something about a particular command or tool that stumps you.

You need to be aware that Corel made *big* changes between the first release of the program and Version E1. Take the time to open Photo-Paint and pull down the Help menu. Look at the About Corel Photo-Paint dialog box and see whether you are using Version 5.00E1 or later. If so, everything should be OK. If not, you need to contact Corel and get the upgrade.

CorelPhoto-Paint 5 Command Reference

You can do some mind-blowing things with CorelPhoto-Paint if you're of a mind to. You only need to master about 88 kabillion different tools and functions, forget quite a bit of what you already know about CorelDraw, and develop a level of patience that would make Job jealous.

If you're willing to take on this burden, you can do neat stuff like put people's heads on other people's bodies and wipe out all the bad physical traits of your beloved in one decisive swipe of a brush. It's fantasy time.

100% (No Zoom)

Displays the image at its normal size.

Digital rodent replacement
Ctrl+1

Acquire Image

⇨ Select Source...
⇨ Acquire...

Pulls in an image from your scanner.

Using Acquire Image

If you have connected a scanner to your computer, you can bring scans directly into Photo-Paint by using this command. Follow these steps:

1. If you have two or more sources for scanned images (Corel Image Source and the one that came with your scanner, for example), first select the one that you want to use by choosing Select Source from the Acquire Image flyout menu under the File menu.

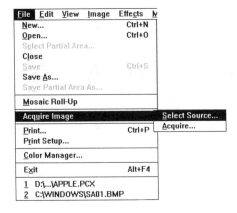

Add To Selection

2. Choose Acquire from the same flyout menu and follow the directions that came with your scanner.

Add To Selection

Adds a new area to an existing mask or complex object.

Using Add To Selection

Before you can use Add To Selection, you must have a selection already in place. To add an additional area to an existing mask:

1. If you haven't created the original mask, create a mask with one of the Mask tools (the second tool flyout from the top in the Tool menu).

2. Choose the Mask tool that you want to use to define the area that you want to add to the original mask: the polygonal or circular Mask tool, for example.

3. Choose Add To Selection from the Special menu.

4. Define the new area with the Mask tool. When you release the mouse button, the new area is added to the mask.

To use Add To Selection to create an even more complex *object* than the one you (supposedly) already have:

1. Choose Build Mode from the Object menu.

 You can also use this button to get into Build Mode.

2. Select one of the Object tools and create a shape.

3. Define another area with the same tool or choose another tool.

4. Choose Create from the Object menu and then choose one of the following from the flyout:

- Copy creates an object that is a copy of the selected areas.

- Cut creates an object that replaces the selected areas.

 You can also use this button to create a copy object.

All (Mask and Object Menus)

More stuff

Where the areas intersect, they are combined. If the areas do not intersect, they become one mask with two separate areas. Nobody ever said that this stuff was easy.

All (Mask and Object Menus)

The All command appears in both the Mask and Object menus. Use the Mask⇨All command to apply a mask to the entire image. Use Object⇨All to select the entire image as a complex object.

A complex object is just a selection of one or more objects created with one of the Object tools.

Using All

To apply a mask to the entire image, choose All from the Mask menu.

To select an entire image as a complex object, choose All from the Object menu.

Arrange Icons

Photo-Paint, unlike Draw, allows you to open several images at the same time. To avoid embarrassing screen clutter, you may want to minimize several of them. The Arrange Icons command puts the icons representing the minimized images in a tidy little line at the bottom of the screen.

Using Arrange Icons

If you have minimized some of your images with the Image window's Control menu, choose Arrange Icons from the Windows menu to line them all up, pretty and ready for inspection, as the following figure demonstrates.

Build Mode 127

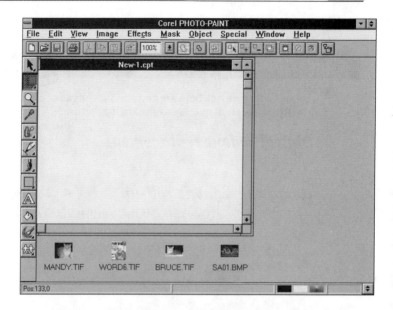

Artistic

⇨ Pointillism...

⇨ Impressionism...

 See Effects & Filters.

Build Mode

Combines several areas that you have defined with the Object tools into one complex object so that you can manipulate them as a unit.

Using Build Mode

You can activate Build Mode in two ways:

- Choose Build Mode from the Object menu. When the command is checked in the menu, Build Mode is active.

 - Click on this button in the ribbon bar.

This button changes its face when you click on it. If the button looks like the preceding one, Build Mode is turned off.

Canvas Roll-Up

 If the button looks like this, Build Mode is active.

Canvas Roll-Up

Applies a texture or a background to your canvas or applies a mostly transparent overlay to an existing picture.

Digital rodent replacement
F3

Using the Canvas roll-up

1. Choose View⇨Canvas Roll-Up to open the Canvas roll-up.

2. To import a canvas, click on the Load button to open the Load a Canvas from Disk dialog box.

3. Find the canvas you want to use by using the dialog box.

   The canvases that come with Photo-Paint are located in the COREL50\PHOTOPNT\CANVAS directory.

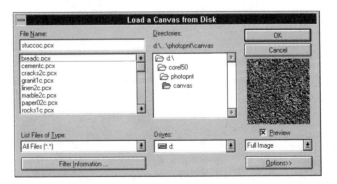

4. If you're using a bitmap image that isn't quite the right size for your canvas, you can choose Crop or Resample from the drop-down list under the Preview checkbox.

If you're going to resize, you need to remember the dimensions that you established when you created the picture (see the following warning in the "More Stuff" section).

5. Click on OK to return to the Canvas roll-up.
6. Set the level of Transparency. High numbers make the canvas more transparent.
7. Set the Emboss level. Embossing gives the canvas a raised-relief effect.
8. Click on the Apply button and go get a cup of coffee. When you get back, the canvas may have been painted with your background choice. Perhaps.
9. If you want the background to become a permanent part of your canvas, click on the Merge button in the Canvas roll-up.

More stuff

You don't have to use the sample textures that come with the program. You can obtain some really interesting results by using a Windows Bitmap (BMP), CompuServe Graphics Interchange (GIF), JPEG (JPG), Photo-CD (PCD), TARGA (TGA), TIFF (TIF), or PCX image.

Watch the file size! It's easy to get so carried away with this canvas trick that your picture grows to many megabytes in size, bringing your system to a rather unpleasant halt.

Cascade

Unlike Draw, Photo-Paint allows you to have several images open at the same time. To avoid the shameful experience of an untidy screen, you may want to cascade all your pictures neatly, one on top of the other. The Cascade command does this trick automatically — using it is a lot easier than picking up your clothes, too.

Digital rodent replacement

Shift+F5

Using Cascade

If you have a deep-seated need to be neat, choose Windows⇨ Cascade to display all your open pictures tidily stacked, as the following figure shows.

130 Checkpoint

Checkpoint

Saves the current image at a given point so that you can return to it with the Restore To Checkpoint command if you change your mind about what you're doing.

Using Checkpoint

Choose Checkpoint from the Edit menu.

More stuff

To go back to the checkpoint if what you're doing doesn't work out, choose Return To Checkpoint from the Edit menu. You can have only one checkpoint at a time.

Clear

Removes the currently selected mask or object from the picture.

Digital rodent replacement

Delete

Using Clear

Select the object or mask that you want to remove and then choose Edit➪Clear.

Close

Closes the current image but leaves Photo-Paint active.

Using Close

Choose File➪Close.

Color

- ➪ Brightness and contrast...
- ➪ Gamma...
- ➪ Hue/saturation...
- ➪ Tone map...

Adjust the picture to make it the best it can be.

Using Color

To adjust the brightness, contrast, and intensity of an image, follow these steps:

1. Choose Brightness and contrast from the Color flyout in the Effects menu to open the Brightness-Contrast-Intensity dialog box.

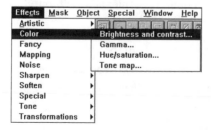

The dialog box opens with a part of your picture in the Preview box. You can point to the picture in the box, click the left mouse button, and drag the image into a more visible location, much the same way that you drag a photo inside a cropping box.

Color

You can also zoom in and out by clicking (not dragging) on the preview area with the left (zoom in) and right (zoom out) mouse buttons.

2. Adjust the sliders to adjust the following:

  - **Brightness:** Lightens or darkens the image.

  - **Contrast:** Changes the difference between light and dark areas.

  - **Intensity:** Makes the bright areas of an image brighter or darker.

3. Click on the Preview button to see whether you have what you want.

4. Click on OK.

To adjust the Gamma value (which enhances midtones by changing the middle gray-scale values without changing either the shadow or highlights), follow these steps:

1. Choose Gamma from the Color flyout in the Effe<u>c</u>ts menu to open the Gamma dialog box.

   Say hello to Mandy, who would very much like to be a tiger.

2. Adjust the slider to increase or decrease the Gamma value.

3. Click on the Preview button to see whether you have what you want.

4. Click on OK.

To adjust hue and saturation, follow these steps:

1. Choose Hue/saturation from the Color flyout in the Effects menu to open the Hue/Saturation dialog box.

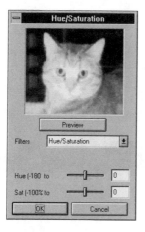

Say hello to Bruce, who *is* a tiger. He's just vertically and horizontally challenged.

2. Adjust the sliders to increase or decrease the Hue (amount of color) and Saturation (amount of color) values.
3. Click on the Preview button to see whether you have what you want.
4. Click on OK.

To adjust the tone map, follow these steps:

1. Choose Tone map from the Color flyout in the Effects menu to open the Tone Map dialog box.

134 Color Correction

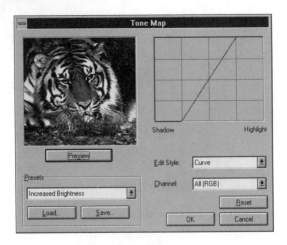

Say hello to Tiger, who — if you're lucky — isn't at all hungry.

2. Play with the presets or drag the handles on the curve to new locations to modify the map.
3. Click on the Preview button to see whether you have what you want.
4. Click on OK.

Color Correction

- ➪ None
- ➪ Fast
- ➪ Accurate
- ➪ Simulate Printer

The Color Correction command increases the accuracy of the way colors appear on-screen. The command takes its direction from your System Color Profile. Selecting None uses no color correction, so it is the fastest. Fast uses some color correction and is a little slower. Accurate uses more color correction, and Simulate Printer, when available, uses the most.

See Color Manager for information about the System Color Profile.

The price you pay for greater accuracy is speed. Unless you have a pretty fast machine with lots of RAM, you probably want to leave this option set at None or Fast.

Color Manager... 135

Using Color Correction

To change the accuracy of your color display, choose View➪Color Correction and then choose either None, Fast, Accurate, or Simulate Printer from the flyout menu.

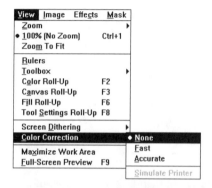

Color Manager...

Creates a System Color Profile for your monitor, scanner, and printer and helps Draw display, acquire, and print colors more accurately. The Color Correction command also uses this profile.

 This command is not for the faint-at-heart or for anyone who does not have the manuals that came with your monitor and printer. If you don't have the manual for the scanner, you can calibrate it by using the target image that comes in the CorelDRAW! 5 manual.

Using Color Manager

To generate a new color profile:

1. Choose Color Manager from the File menu. The System Color Profile dialog box opens.

2. Select your Monitor, Printer, and Scanner from the drop-down lists.

   If your monitor, printer, or scanner does not appear in the drop-down list, choose Other. This option opens a Calibration dialog box that allows you to enter information about the device and calibrate it for optimal use in your system.

3. Select the default color-matching method:

   - **AutoMatch:** This is your best choice. AutoMatch determines whether you are printing a vector or bitmapped object and applies either the photographic or

Color Manager...

> **System Color Profile**
>
> Current Profile: ray.ccs
>
> Notes:
>
> Monitor: NEC MultiSync 5FG [Edit...]
> Printer: HP DeskJet 550/560 [Edit...]
> Scanner: HP ScanJet 2C [Edit...]
>
> ⦿ AutoMatch ○ Photographic ○ Illustration
>
> [Select] [Generate] [Cancel]
>
> Hints
> A System Color Profile studies your monitor, scanner and printer to more accurately capture, display and print color. When possible, use the list to choose your device, since these are tested settings. Use Automatch as your default color matching method, unless you need to force Photographic or Illustration color matching. Depending on the device(s) selected, it can take from 10 to 20 minutes to generate a profile.

illustration gamut-mapping system. (Gamut-mapping is the way your printer is told to reproduce colors that are outside its printing capabilities.)

- **Photographic:** When you choose this option, all gamut-mapping is done by using the photographic mapping system, regardless of object type.

- **Illustration:** When you choose this option, all gamut-mapping is done by using the illustration mapping system, regardless of object type.

To select an existing color profile:

1. Choose Color Manager from the File menu. The System Color Profile dialog box opens.

2. Select the profile you want from the Current Profile drop-down list.

3. Click on the Select button.

To edit an existing color profile:

1. Choose Color Manager from the File menu. The System Color Profile dialog box opens.

2. Select the profile you want to edit from the Current Profile drop-down list (if not already active).

3. Click on the Edit button next to the component you want to change.

4. Enter revised information, or recalibrate the device, in the Calibration dialog box.

Color Mask Roll-Up

 Depending on the amount of memory and the speed of your machine, Color Manager can take a long time to develop a profile — on CompuServe, one person reported an instance in which it took two hours to complete. More common are generation times in the 10- to 30-minute range.

Color Mask Roll-Up

Use this roll-up to select a range of colors to modify or protect from change.

Digital rodent replacement

F4

Using the Color Mask roll-up

To select a range of colors to modify or protect:

1. Choose Color Mask Roll-Up from the Mask menu.

2. In the Color Mask roll-up, choose either Protect Selected Colors or Modify Selected Colors from the drop-down list.

3. Turn on a color by selecting the first unchecked On checkbox.

4. Click on the button next to the On checkbox. The cursor turns into an eyedropper shape.

5. Click on the color that you want to modify or protect. The button in the roll-up changes to match the selected color.

Color Roll-Up

6. To increase or decrease the range of shades of the color that you select, change the tolerance levels in the scroll boxes.

7. To see the areas to be selected, click on the Preview Mask button.

8. Repeat steps 3 through 7 for any additional colors (up to ten) that you want to mask.

9. Click on Apply to create the mask that either allows the colors to be changed or protects them.

More stuff

The mask that you create is invisible. However, the colors you select are the only ones acted on, or protected from change, in subsequent actions.

Color Roll-Up

Choose paint and background colors with this roll-up.

Digital rodent replacement

F2

Using the Color roll-up

1. Choose View➪Color Roll-Up.

2. If you know the values of the color you want, enter them in the Color Components boxes in the roll-up and skip to step 5.

— Color Components boxes
— Color Model drop-down listbox

Color Roll-Up 139

TIP

The three scroll boxes located along the top of the Color roll-up are called *Color Component boxes*. They change titles with the color model you're using: RGB for the red, green, and blue model, CMY for the cyan, magenta, yellow, and black model, and so on.

3. Select the color model you want to use from the Color Model drop-down listbox:

   - **RGB:** Red, green, and blue
   - **CMY:** Cyan, magenta, yellow, and black
   - **HSB:** Hue, saturation, and brightness
   - **LAB:** Luminosity of green to magenta and of blue to yellow
   - **Image Palette:** Colors in the current image
   - **Gray:** Shades of gray. This option is available only when you're editing transparency masks.

4. Select the paint or paper color (the documentation also refers to the color called *paper* as *background*) by clicking on one of the boxes next to the Color Model listbox. The cursor changes to an eyedropper. Then click the eyedropper on the color you want to use.

5. The selected color is active when you use the next Paint tool.

More stuff

Additional options are available from the flyout menu that appears when you click on the flyout menu button under the Color Model box.

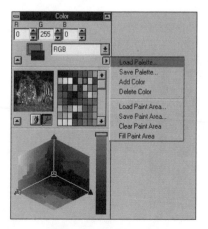

Color Tolerance...

- **Load Palette:** Selects a different palette.
- **Save Palette:** Saves the current palette so you can use it later.
- **Add Color:** Saves the color displayed in the Paint or Paper boxes (depending on which one is active) and adds it to the color table.
- **Delete Color:** Deletes the color displayed in the Paint or Paper boxes (depending on which one is active).
- **Load Paint Area:** Loads a BMP file so that you can select colors from it. When the bitmap is displayed, you can click on any of its colors whenever the eyedropper cursor is active.
- **Save Paint Area:** Saves the current paint area as a bitmap file.
- **Clear Paint Area:** Clears the paint area and fills it with the currently selected paper or background color.
- **Fill Paint Area:** Fills the paint area with a selection of colors so you can pick them with the eyedropper.

Color Tolerance...

Establishes the range of shades of a color that is selected with the Magic Wand tool or a Fill tool.

Using Color Tolerance

To increase or decrease the range of shades selected with the Magic Wand or a Fill tool:

1. Choose Color Tolerance from the Special menu to open the Color Comparison Tolerance dialog box.

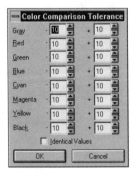

Convert To

2. To change the range of colors selected or replaced, enter color values in the boxes. Higher plus and minus numbers represent more shades. The range can be 0 to 255.

3. To make all selections the same, click on the Identical Values checkbox.

4. The new values apply the next time you use a Fill tool or the Magic Wand.

Combine Channels...

Puts back together channels that you split with the Split Channels To command.

 See Split Channels To find out how to split an image into its color channels.

Using Combine Channels

To recombine an image after it has been split into its color channels for editing:

1. Choose Combine Channels from the Image menu.

2. Check that the channels appear in the proper order in the Channels dialog box (the red .TIF file next to the R, the blue .TIF file next to the B, and so on).

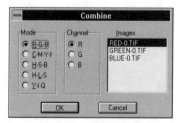

3. Click on OK.

Convert To

- ⇨ Black and White
- ⇨ Line Art
- ⇨ Printer Halftone

Copy

⇨ Screen Halftone
⇨ 16 Colors
⇨ Grayscale
⇨ 256 Colors
⇨ RGB Color
⇨ CYMK Color

Converts an image to another color format.

Using Convert To

1. Make the image that you want to convert active.
2. Choose Image⇨Convert To.
3. Select the new color format from the flyout menu.

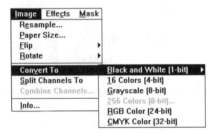

4. Photo-Paint color-converts the image and opens it in a new window.

More stuff

The current image's format is grayed out in the menu list.

Copy

Copying an object or a mask makes a duplicate of it and places the duplicate on the Windows Clipboard.

Digital rodent replacement

 Click this button or press Ctrl+C.

Using Copy

Select the object or mask to copy and then choose Edit⇨Copy.

Create (Object Menu) 143

More stuff

After you copy the object to the Clipboard, you can paste it into most Windows applications simply by choosing Paste from the application's Edit menu.

Copy To File...

Copies an object or a mask and makes a duplicate of it by saving it to a file on disk.

Using Copy To File

1. Select the object or mask to copy to a file.
2. Choose Copy To File from the Edit menu.
3. Enter the File Name, Type, and Directory in the Save an Image to Disk dialog box.

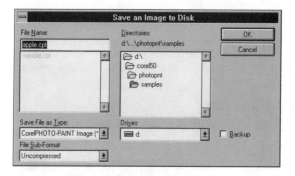

4. If you want a backup copy, check the Backup checkbox.
5. Click on OK.

Create (Object Menu)

⇨ Copy

⇨ Cut

Creates objects out of areas that you have assembled by using Build Mode.

Create Brush...

Using Create

1. With Build Mode active, select the areas of the image that you want to make into an object with one or more of the Object tools.
2. Choose Object⇨Create.
3. If you want to copy the areas as a new object, choose Copy from the Create flyout menu.

If you want to cut the selected areas into a new object, choose Cut from the Create flyout menu. The areas that you cut from the image assume the color assigned to Paper.

 ## More stuff

This command works only with objects.

Create Brush...

Makes a custom-shaped brush out of a defined mask area.

Using Create Brush

To create a brush with a custom shape:

1. Define the brush shape by using Mask tools.
2. Choose Create Brush from the Special menu.
3. Select a brush size in the Create a Brush dialog box.

Create Transparency Mask 145

4. Click on OK.

More stuff

The new brush is added to the end of the Custom Brush area of the Tool Settings roll-up.

Create Transparency Mask

⇨ New...
⇨ From Mask...

Normal masks protect the underlying image from change. Transparent masks vary the amount of protection with the amount of transparency. When you make a mask more transparent, it provides less protection.

Using Create Transparency Mask

Creating masks can take a lot of time. Be sure that the coffee pot is plugged in and that you have some time that you want to devote to meditation or isometric exercises before you start creating them.

To create a transparency mask over the entire image:

1. Choose New from the Create Transparency Mask flyout menu in the Mask menu.

2. If you want the transparency mask to have the same level of transparency throughout, click on the Uniform radio button in the Transparency Mask Creation dialog box.

Crop Image

3. Enter a number between 1 and 255 to represent the amount of transparency you want. The higher the number, the more transparent the mask becomes and the less protection it gives to an underlying image.

4. Click on OK to apply the mask.

 If you want the mask to vary in the amount of protection it offers, choose Gradient in the Transparency Mask Creation dialog box and then select the pattern you want from the drop-down listbox.

The darker the colors appear in the preview box, the more protection the mask offers.

To create a transparency mask from a regular mask:

1. Define a mask area with one of the Mask tools.

2. Choose From Mask from the Create Transparency Mask flyout menu in the Mask menu.

3. Enter a number between 1 and 100 to designate the amount of transparency.

4. Enter a number between 1 and 100 to set the amount of feathering. (*Feathering* blends the edges of the mask with the underlying image.)

5. Click on OK.

More stuff

You can change the gradient of a gradient transparency mask by using the Fill roll-up and the Layers/Objects roll-up. First, choose Edit Transparency from the Layers/Objects roll-up. Then fill the mask with a gradient fill from the Fill roll-up.

You can also edit other aspects of the transparent mask when it is open in the Layers/Objects roll-up. Use any tool in the toolbox to customize the mask to your liking.

Transparency masks can be saved to be used again and again. Choose Save Transparency Mask from the Mask menu.

Crop Image

Crops a picture to the outline of a mask.

Using Crop Image

Draw a mask that defines the area that you want to include in the cropped image. Then choose Crop Image from the Mask menu.

More stuff

 If the mask has been inverted, the crop area is the area outside the mask.

See Invert for more information.

Cut

Cutting an object removes the object or mask and places it on the Windows Clipboard.

Digital rodent replacement

Ctrl+X

Ribbon bar icon

Using Cut

Select the object or mask to cut and then choose Edit⇨Cut.

More stuff

After you cut the object to the Clipboard, you can paste it into most Windows applications simply by choosing Paste from the application's Edit menu.

Delete

Deleting an object removes it *without* placing a copy on the Windows Clipboard.

Digital rodent replacement

Delete

Using Delete

Select the object to delete and then choose Object⇨Delete.

148 Distort

Distort

Adjusts the placement, size, scale, angle of rotation, and skew of a selected object. Same dialog box and concept as the Transform roll-up in CorelDraw, except it applies to an object.

Using the Distort (Tool Settings) roll-up

The five buttons that run along the top of the roll-up control the various functions of the command. They are Place, Rotate, Scale and Mirror, Size, and Skew.

To oh-so-precisely place an object in a drawing or move it about exactly so much, follow these steps:

1. Select the object the you want to place or move.
2. Choose Distort from the Object menu.
 3. Click on the Place button to open the Placement commands.
4. If you want to move the object horizontally or vertically by a specific amount, check the Relative Position box.
5. Enter measurements in the H (Horizontal) and V (Vertical) boxes. If the Relative Position box is checked, enter the amount of movement you want from the current position. If the Relative Position box is not checked, enter the measurements from the ruler where you want the object to be placed.
6. Click on Apply to apply the placement to the object, or click on Apply To Duplicate to create a new object at the specified position.

To rotate an object in a drawing, follow these steps:

1. Select the object that you want to rotate.
2. Choose Object⇨Distort.
 3. Click on the Rotate button to open the Rotation commands.

Distort 149

4. Enter the angle of rotation you want in the Angle Of Rotation box (positive numbers rotate the object counter-clockwise, and negative numbers rotate it clockwise).

5. Click on Apply to apply the rotation to the object or click on Apply To Duplicate to create a new object with the specified rotation.

To scale an object in a drawing, follow these steps:

1. Select the object that you want to scale.
2. Choose Distort from the Object menu.

3. Click on the Scale button to access the Scale commands.

4. Enter the percentages of scale you want in H and V boxes. To maintain the object's aspect, enter identical measurements in the H and V boxes. To stretch the object, enter a larger or smaller number in one or the other.

All this stuff is bunches easier, if somewhat less precise, with the mouse. Click on the object until the selection handles appear, and then drag the corner handles to scale the object or the side handles to stretch it.

5. If you want to mirror the object, press the horizontal or vertical mirror button or both.

6. Click on Apply to apply the scale to the object or click on Apply To Duplicate to create a new object with the specified size.

To precisely size an object, follow these steps:

1. Select the object that you want to size.
2. Choose Distort from the Object menu.

3. Click on the Size button to open the scale commands.

4. Enter the new measurements in the H and V boxes.

You can do so with the mouse. Click on the object until the selection handles appear, and then drag the corner handles to scale the object or the side handles to stretch it. Check out the status line while you're dragging or scaling. The percentage of change is shown, giving you a pretty good guidepost.

5. Click on Apply to apply the size to the object or click on Apply To Duplicate to create a new object with the specified size.

To precisely skew an object, follow these steps:

150 Duplicate

1. Select the object that you want to squish.
2. Choose Distort from the Object menu.

3. Click on the Skew button to open the Skew commands.
4. Enter the amount of skew you want in the H and V boxes.

You can perform this operation with the mouse, too. Double-click on the object until the rotation arrows appear and then drag one of the four side handles to skew the object. Check out the status line while you're skewing to see the skew angle.

5. Click on Apply to apply the skew to the object, or click on Apply To Duplicate to create a new object with the specified skew.

More stuff

You can select the unit of measurement used in the Distort roll-up in the General section of the Preferences dialog box.

Duplicate

Creates a copy of the selected object(s).

Digital rodent replacement
Ctrl+D

Using Duplicate
Select the object that you want to duplicate and then choose Duplicate from the Object menu.

More stuff
If you duplicate by pressing Ctrl+D or by selecting the Duplicate command from the Object menu, the copy of the object is placed a little below and to the right of the original. You can nudge the duplicate about with the arrow keys.

Exit

Quits Corel Photo-Paint and returns you to wherever you started the program (to either the Windows Program Manager or the File Manager).

Digital rodent replacement

Alt+F4

More stuff

When you choose File➪Exit without saving open images first, a dialog box appears and asks whether you want to save your work. To save the stuff, choose Yes; the image is saved if it is already named, or the Save As dialog box appears if you have not saved the drawing before. To abandon the changes, choose No.

Effects & Filters

Photo-Paint provides oodles of different filters and effects to twist images in a multitude of interesting ways. You can access them in the Effects menu and in various dialog boxes throughout the program.

You can view the effects of the filter in the Preview box associated with each one. A brief explanation of each filter follows.

You can zoom in and out in most Preview boxes by using the left and right mouse buttons. Also, the cursor changes into a hand when positioned in the box, and you can drag the image about in the Preview box to get a better look at it.

Artistic

- **Pointillism:** Adds a series of multicolored dots.
- **Impressionism:** Applies different styles of brushstrokes.

Color

Refer to Color for options.

Fancy

- **Edge Detect:** Creates an outline effect.
- **Emboss:** Creates a raised-relief effect.
- **Invert:** Creates a photo-negative effect.
- **Jaggy Despeckle:** Scatters colors and smoothes jagged edges.
- **Motion Blur:** Creates movement blur.
- **Outline:** Traces the edges of the image.

Effects & Filters

Mapping

- **Glass Block:** Makes the image look like it is behind a series of glass blocks.
- **Impressionist:** Makes the image look like an impressionist oil painting.
- **Map to Sphere:** Wraps the image around a sphere or cylinder.
- **Pinch/Punch:** Makes the image appear pinched in or punched out.
- **Pixelate:** Adds a blocklike effect to the image.
- **Ripple:** Adds a wave effect. (Drink enough and you add a blackout effect.)
- **Smoked Glass:** Makes the image appear as though it is behind smoked glass.
- **Swirl:** Rotates the image à la soft ice cream.
- **Tile:** Creates a pattern composed of tiles of the image.
- **Vignette:** Adds soft light around the center of image.
- **Wet Paint:** Makes the image look drippy.
- **Wind:** Makes object look windblown.

Noise

- **Add Noise:** Adds texture.
- **Gaussian:** Scatters the colors.
- **Spike:** Creates a thinner texture.
- **Uniform:** Creates an even texture.
- **Maximum:** Lightens the image and decreases the number of colors.
- **Median:** Removes noise (think of a fuzzy TV picture) from scanned images.
- **Minimum:** Darkens the image and decreases the number of colors.
- **Remove Noise:** Softens edges and reduces the speckled effect.

Sharpen

- **Adaptive Unsharp:** Reveals edge detail without messing with the rest of the picture.

- **Directional Sharpen:** Applies different amounts of sharpening across the image.
- **Edge Enhance:** Highlights edges.
- **Enhance:** Highlights or smoothes edges.
- **Sharpen:** Highlights edges and brings out detail.
- **Unsharp Mask:** Sharpens smooth areas in a picture and accentuates edge detail.

Soften

- **Diffuse:** Scatters colors.
- **Directional Smooth:** Evens out differences in adjacent pixels.
- **Smooth:** Lessens harshness.
- **Soften:** Smoothes and softens colors.

Special

- **Contour:** Outlines the edge of the picture.
- **Posterize:** Creates areas of solid colors or shades of gray.
- **Psychedelic:** Far out, man.
- **Solarize:** Creates a negative image of pixels in the picture.
- **Threshold:** Gradually darkens the image.

Tone

- **Equalize:** Makes color corrections.

Transformations

- **3D Rotate:** Rotates the image in three dimensions.
- **Mesh Warp:** Stretches and distorts the image to conform to wire mesh.
- **Perspective:** Applies a perspective effect.

Fill Roll-Up

Use to select color and fill patterns to apply with the Fill tool.

Fill Roll-Up

Digital rodent replacement
Shift+F6

Using the Fill roll-up

To select a uniform color fill:

1. Choose Fill Roll-Up from the View menu.
2. Click on the color wheel button to open the uniform fill selection area.

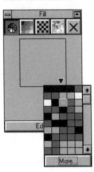

3. Click on the preview area to open the color selection area.
4. Choose the uniform color you want from this area, or click on the Edit button to open the Uniform Fill dialog box to mix your own custom color.

The current paint, paper, and fill colors appear along the bottom right of the screen. You can open the Fill dialog box by double-clicking on the fill color.

To select a fountain fill:

1. Choose Fill Roll-Up from the View menu.
2. Click on the fountain fill button to open the fountain fill selection area.

3. Click on the linear, circular, conical, or square button.

Fill Roll-Up 155

4. Select the starting and ending colors.
5. To build your own fill, click on the Edit button to open the Fountain Fill dialog box.

For a discussion of the Fountain Fill dialog box, see Fountain Fill in Part I.

You can modify the fill pattern by clicking in the preview area and dragging the crosshairs that appears to a new position. In the case of a conical fill, you can also change the location of the highlighted area by using the right mouse button to relocate it.

To select a bitmap fill:

1. Choose Fill Roll-Up from the View menu.
2. Click on the bitmap fill button to open the bitmap fill selection area.

3. Click on the Load button to open the normal fill selection area.
4. Select the bitmap image that you want to use as a fill.

You can use any bitmap image as a fill. Photo-Paint comes with a wide variety of examples, which are located in the COREL50\PHOTOPNT\TILES directory.

To select a texture fill:

1. Choose Fill Roll-Up from the View menu.
2. Click on the texture fill button to open the texture fill selection area.

3. Click in the preview area to open thumbnails of the available fills in the current library, or select a texture from the textures list.
4. To roll your own texture, click on the Edit button.

More stuff

You apply fills, once selected, with the Fill tool.

Flip

⇨ Horizontally
⇨ Vertically

When you select it from the Object menu, this command flips the selected object either Horizontally or Vertically. When selected from the Image menu, it flips the entire image either Horizontally or Vertically.

Font...

Selects the font and effects.

Using Font

1. Choose Font from the Edit menu.
2. Choose the Font, Font Style, Size, and Effects in the Font dialog box.

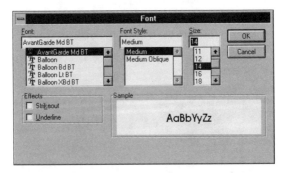

3. Click on OK.

Invert (Mask Menu and Object Menu)

Full-Screen Preview

Lets you see the image in its full-screen glory without the distraction of menus and the like.

Digital rodent replacement
F9

Using Full-Screen Preview

Choose Full-Screen Preview from the View menu. Press any key to return to normal view.

Info...

Shows the following image information: name, width, height, DPI in both X-axis (horizontal) and Y-axis (vertical), type, size, format, number of objects, and whether the image has changed.

Using Info

Choose Info from the Image menu. Click on OK to close the information box.

Invert (Mask Menu and Object Menu)

Reverses the selection, selecting everything that was not selected and deselecting all that was originally selected.

Using Invert

To invert a mask:

1. Create the mask by using the Mask tools.

2. Choose Invert from the Mask menu for a regular mask or Invert Transparency Mask for a transparency mask.

 Transparency masks are not either on or off like regular masks are. Instead, they provide variable protection to the underlying image. Inverting a transparency mask reverses its effect. What was only slightly protected becomes pretty heavily protected, and what was pretty heavily protected becomes only slightly so.

Layers/Objects Roll-Up

To invert an object:

1. Create the object by using Build Mode and the Object tools or by pasting an image from the Clipboard.
2. Select the object with the Object Picker tool.
3. Choose Invert from the Object menu.
4. Choose Create from the Object menu or click on the Create Object button on the toolbar.

Layers/Objects Roll-Up

Controls the editing and positioning of objects.

Digital rodent replacement
Ctrl+F7

Using the Layers/Objects roll-up

To edit a transparency:

1. Create a transparent mask.
2. Choose Layers/Objects Roll-Up from the Object menu to display the roll-up.

3. Click on the Edit Transparency radio button. The transparency becomes visible. You can now use the Effects and Paint tools to edit the mask.

Load... (Mask, Transparency Mask)

To edit an image:

1. Choose Layers/Objects Roll-Up from the Object menu.
2. Click on the Edit Image radio button.
3. You can edit individual channels (red, green, blue, or all) by selecting the channel from the drop-down list.

To edit individual objects:

1. Choose Layers/Objects Roll-Up from the Object menu.

   The Drawing Mode box shows a representation of each object in the image. To show or hide the object, click on the button that represents it.

2. Hide all objects but the one you want to edit.
3. Make your changes to the object, including editing color channels.
4. Click on the Show All button to see the results.

To change the order of objects in an image and adjust the amount of opacity and feathering:

1. Choose Layers/Objects Roll-Up from the Object menu.
2. Highlight the object that you want to reorder by using the Object Picker tool.
3. Click on one of the Order buttons to rearrange. The buttons are

    - ⬆ Moves the selected object to the front.
    - ⌃ Moves the selected object forward one.
    - ⌄ Moves the selected object back one.
    - ⬇ Moves the selected object to the rear.

4. Adjust the Opacity and Feathering sliders to make the image more or less transparent and merge its outline with the underlying layer.

Load... (Mask, Transparency Mask)

After you create a mask, you can name and save it as a file by using the Save and Save Transparency Mask commands in the Mask menu. The Load and Load Transparency Mask commands recall the saved mask to be used again.

Using Load and Load Transparency Mask

To reuse a saved mask:

1. Choose Load or Load Transparency Mask from the Mask menu.
2. Select the desired mask from the resulting directory tree dialog box.
3. Click on OK.

Mapping

See Effects & Filters.

Marquee Visible

Toggles the display of marquee boxes around objects on and off.

Using Marquee Visible

To toggle the display of marquee boxes on or off, choose Marquee Visible from the Object menu. If the command is checked, the boxes are turned on.

Maximize Work Area

Expands the work area to the max and hides the menus.

Using Maximize Work Area

Choose Maximize Work Area from the View menu.

More stuff

To restore the screen so that menus are again visible, press Alt+V to display the View menu and then choose Restore Screen.

Merge

This command acts like super glue. Selecting an object and then choosing Merge makes the object an inseparable part of the image.

Mosaic Roll-Up

Digital rodent replacement
Ctrl+G

Using Merge
Select the object with the Object Picker tool and then choose Merge from the Object menu.

More stuff
Objects that have been merged together cannot be separated.

Mosaic Roll Up

This roll-up would be really neat if only it would support more file types. It is a visual archive of files on your system that you can drag and drop into a drawing.

Digital rodent replacement
Alt+F1

Using the Mosaic roll-up

1. Choose Mosaic Roll-Up from the File menu.

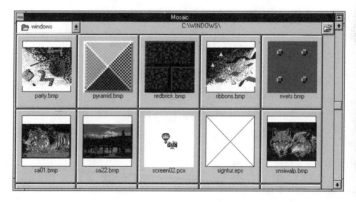

2. Click on the file folder icon in the upper-right corner of the Mosaic window to open the Open Collection dialog box.

New

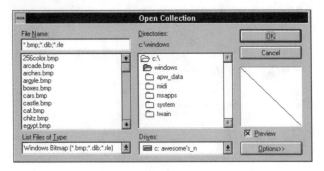

3. Select Drive, Directory, and File Type in the proper areas.
4. The selected images appear in the Mosaic window.
5. To use an image, drag it into your drawing.

More stuff

Clicking on the Options button opens an area that you can use to search for keywords. The Options area also displays notes that have been attached to a graphic and fonts used in the graphic.

New

Opens a new drawing area.

Digital rodent replacement

Ctrl+N

Using New

1. Choose New from the File menu.
2. Choose a Color Mode from the drop-down list in the Create a New Image dialog box.
3. Choose Paper color.
4. Choose Width, Height, and Resolution measurements.
5. Choose the Create as Partial File checkbox if the new image should be part of a larger one.
6. Click on OK.

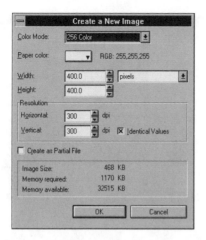

Noise

See Effe**c**ts & Filters.

Open

Loads a drawing into Photo-Paint.

Digital rodent replacement

Ctrl+O

Ribbon bar icon

Using **O**pen

1. Choose **O**pen from the **F**ile menu.
2. Enter the filename in the File **N**ame box or use the Dri**v**es and **D**irectories boxes to locate the drawing. A thumbnail representation of the contents of the template appears in the preview area if you select the **P**review checkbox.

164 Paper Size...

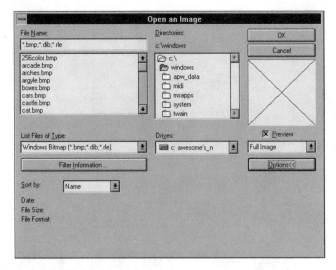

3. Click on OK.

More stuff

You can use wildcards in the File Name box. For example, entering **ex*.*** displays a list of all files beginning with *ex* in the selected directory.

Paper Size...

Sets the size of the paper (background).

Using Paper Size

To change the size of the paper:

1. Choose Paper Size from the Image menu.

2. Enter the new measurements for the paper size in the Width and Height boxes.

If you want to maintain the aspect of the paper, check the Maintain Aspect checkbox and enter only the Width or the Height measurement.

3. From the Placement drop-down list, select the place at which you want the current image to be placed on the new paper.

You can manually adjust the placement by moving the image in the preview box. Put the cursor in the box, and it changes into the hand shape. Then click the left mouse button and drag the image to the desired position.

4. Click on OK.

The Paper Size command specifies the size of the background. It has no effect on the image.

Paste

- ⇨ As New Object
- ⇨ As New Document

Pastes Clipboard contents into an image or as a new image file.

Digital rodent replacement
Ctrl+V (As New Object)

Ribbon bar icon

Using Paste

1. Make sure that the object or mask that you want to paste into Photo-Paint is on the Windows Clipboard.
2. Choose Paste from the Edit menu or click on the Paste icon in the toolbar.
3. To bring the mask or object from the Clipboard into the current Photo-Paint image, choose As New Object from the Paste flyout menu.

   To bring the mask or object from the Clipboard into a new Photo-Paint image, choose As New Document from the Paste flyout menu.

Paste From File...

Pastes the contents of a file into an image.

Using Paste From File

1. Choose Paste From File from the Edit menu.
2. Find the image that you want to import in the Paste an Image from Disk dialog box.

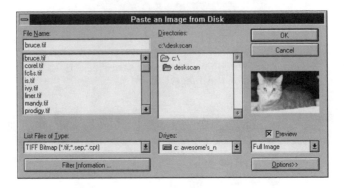

3. Click on OK.

Preferences...

Sets startup and color defaults.

Digital rodent replacement
Ctrl+J

Using Preferences

1. Choose Preferences from the Special menu.
2. Click on the General tab in the Preferences dialog box to make the following changes:

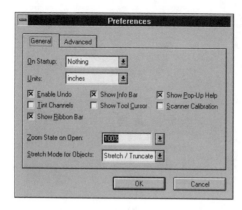

- **On Startup:** Select from the drop-down list how you want Photo-Paint to start: with nothing open, with a new window open, or with the Open File dialog box active.
- **Units:** Select your favorite measurement unit to be used in the dialog boxes and on the rulers.
- Check the appropriate boxes for the stuff that you want to show on-screen at startup.
- **Zoom State on Open:** Select a percentage from the drop-down listbox (Best fit is a good choice).

3. Click on the Advanced tab to choose marquee box colors and the directory for plug-ins.

Print...

Lets you print all or part of your document. You can also make a ton of different selections for the way you document prints, controlling color separations, reference marks, layout, and more.

Digital rodent replacement
Ctrl+P

Ribbon bar icon

Using Print

1. Choose Print from the File menu.
2. Select the desired options in the Print dialog box:

Print...

[Print dialog box shown with Print Range options: All, Selected Objects, Current Page, Pages; Printer: LM WinJet 1200 PS, WinSpool; Printer Quality: 1200 dpi; Printer Color Profile - Generic CMYK Color Printer; Print to File; For Mac; Copies: 1; Collate Copies; buttons OK, Cancel, Setup..., Options...]

- **All:** Prints the whole banana.
- **Selected Objects:** Prints only the selected objects.
- **Current Page:** Prints only the page in the view window.
- **Pages:** Specify the range of pages you want to print — separate individual pages with a comma, stipulate a range in the form **3-5**, or mix and match: **1-3,4,7,45** prints pages 1, 2, 3, 4, 7, and 45.

If you want to print every other page, use the tilde (~). Telling CorelDraw to print **1~** results in all odd-numbered pages printing, **2~** prints all even-numbered pages, and **1~13** prints all odd-numbered pages between 1 and 13.

- **Printer:** Shows the active printer from the Printer Control Panel. Choose any installed printer from the drop-down list.
- **Printer Quality:** If your printer supports this feature, choose the resolution you want.
- **Printer Color Profile:** Shows the current color profile.
- **Print to File:** Creates a file that can be printed from DOS.
- **For Mac:** If you have a PostScript printer, you can print to a file that a Macintosh computer can read and print.
- **Collate Copies:** Collates your documents.
- **Copies:** Allows you to print as many as 999 copies of the drawing.

Using the Print Options dialog box

Clicking on the Print Options... button in the Print dialog box opens the following additional dialog box:

Print... 169

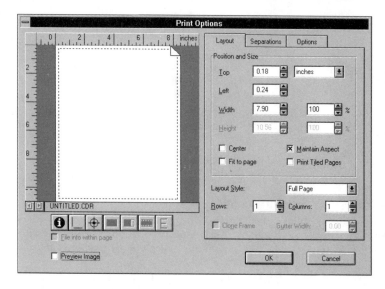

The row of icons directly below the Preview window allows you to add standard printer's marks to a drawing. They are as follows, from left to right:

- Prints filename, current date and time, and tile and plate number on every printable page. Also includes other stuff, like color profile, color name, and screen frequency on color separations.
- Prints crop marks.
- Prints registration marks.
- Prints a calibration bar (RGBCYM).
- Prints densitometer scale on each page.
- Creates a reversed image of the drawing to an image directly on film.
- If your printer or service bureau wants film printed emulsion side down, click on this button.

Layout tab

✔ The Position and Size section allows you to adjust the drawing's size and position on the page.

✔ Selecting the Maintain Aspect box resizes the drawing when printed.

Print Setup...

- Print Tiled Pages prints the parts of the drawing that extend beyond the printable page on separate pages (useful for posters and signs).

- If you are proofing really small stuff, you can use Fit to page to blow the critter up so you can see it more easily.

- Enter values in the Rows, Columns, and Gutter Width boxes to divide the printed page into segments, and check the Clone Frame box to copy the contents of one segment to all the others.

- The Layout Style drop-down list lets you select from the predefined styles. See Page Setup for more information.

Separations tab

- Checking the Print Separations box prints the colors (usually CMYK and any spot colors) in gray-scale separations. Click on the colors that you want to separate in the Colors area.

- The In Color checkbox, when checked, prints the separations in color. This option is available only if you're printing to a file or to a color printer.

- Leave the Use Custom Halftone box unchecked unless you're really advanced at determining halftone screen angles and frequencies. The same goes for the Edit button, which you use to make custom modifications to those angles and frequencies.

- Auto Trapping adds trap to certain objects.

Options tab

Screen Frequency determines the halftone screen frequency used to print the drawing.

More stuff

Don't be overly concerned if your preview area remains blank. I think that Corel's programmers went to lunch when this bit of code was being developed, but everything still prints OK.

Print Setup...

Selects the printer that will print the drawing.

Remove (Remove Transparency Mask) 171

Using P<u>r</u>int Setup

1. Choose P<u>r</u>int Setup from the <u>F</u>ile menu.
2. Select a printer from the list of installed printers in the Print Setup dialog box.

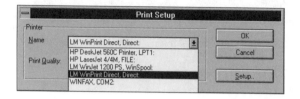

3. Designate the Print Quality if the selected printer has the capability to print at differing resolutions.
4. Click on <u>S</u>etup to open the Windows printer setup dialog box that is specific to the selected printer.

More stuff

See *Windows 3.1 For Dummies, Second Edition* for an explanation of the Control Panel, Printers dialog box.

<u>R</u>efresh

Photo-Paint may leave little bug tracks or other droppings behind every now and again. The <u>R</u>efresh command forces a redraw of the screen and makes Photo-Paint clean up after itself.

Digital rodent replacement

Ctrl+W

Using <u>R</u>efresh

Choose <u>R</u>efresh from the <u>W</u>indow menu.

R<u>e</u>move (R<u>e</u>move Transparency Mask)

Removes masks from the current image.

Using Remove

Choose Remove or Remove Transparency Mask from the Mask menu to remove masks from the image.

Remove From Selection

Takes away an area from a defined complex object or mask.

Ribbon bar icon

Using Remove From Selection

1. Create a mask or complex object.
2. Choose a Mask tool or Object tool.
3. Choose Remove From Selection from the Special menu.
4. Define the area to be removed with your Mask or Object tool.

Remove Transparency Mask

Removes transparency masks from the current image.

Using Remove Transparency Mask

Choose Remove Transparency Mask from the Mask menu to remove transparency masks from the image.

Resample...

Increases or decreases the size and/or resolution of an image.

Using Resample

To change an open image's size and/or resolution, follow these steps:

1. Open the image you want to resample.
2. Choose Resample from the Image menu.
3. Enter values for Units, Width, Height, and Resolution in the Resample dialog box.

Restore To Checkpoint 173

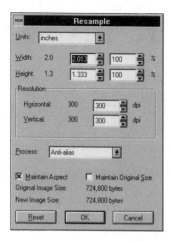

 To maintain the existing aspect of the image after it has been resampled, check the Maintain Aspect checkbox and enter only one measurement in the Width or Height area.

More stuff

You can also do some resampling on an image when you first open it. In the Open an Image dialog box, the drop-down list directly under the Preview box contains a Resample option. Selecting this option opens a Resample dialog box that allows you to decrease the size of the image or its resolution when opening the image file. Proportional dimensions are always maintained.

Restore To Checkpoint

When you change your mind about what you're doing and want to discard changes that you made to an image, Restore To Checkpoint returns you to the last place at which you established a checkpoint with the Checkpoint command.

Using Restore To Checkpoint

 Choose Restore To Checkpoint from the Edit menu.

See the Checkpoint command.

Rotate

Rotate

⇨ 90° Clockwise
⇨ 90° Counterclockwise
⇨ 180°
⇨ Custom… (Free)

The Rotate command is found in both the Object and Image menus. It rotates only the selected object when you access it from the Object menu, and it rotates the entire image when you select it from the Image menu.

Using Rotate

1. Select the object that you want to rotate, or make the image active.
2. Choose Rotate from the appropriate menu.
3. Select the amount and direction of rotation you want from the flyout menu.

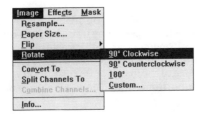

More stuff

To customize the amount of rotation for an image, choose Custom from the Rotate flyout menu and enter the amount of rotation and direction in the dialog box. To customize the amount of rotation of an object, choose Free from the Rotate dialog box, which opens the Tool Settings roll-up. Then follow these steps:

1. Click on the Rotate button to open the rotation commands if they are not already active.
2. Enter the angle of rotation you want in the Angle Of Rotation box (positive numbers rotate the object counterclockwise, and negative numbers rotate it clockwise).
3. Click on Apply to apply the rotation to the object, or click on Apply To Duplicate to create a new object with the specified rotation.

You can rotate the object by double-clicking on it until the rotate/skew handles (arrows) appear. Drag the corner handles to rotate the object; the status line gives you a readout of the amount of rotation you're applying.

Rulers

Toggles the display of the rulers on and off.

Digital rodent replacement

Ctrl+R

Using Rulers

Choose Rulers from the View menu to toggle the display of rulers on and off.

More stuff

You can set the unit of measurement in the General tab of the Preferences dialog box (Ctrl+J).

Save, Save As...

These commands save a document to disk. When you save a document for the first time, the Save an Image to Disk dialog box opens to let you name the document. All subsequent saves use the same name, and the dialog box does not open. You can also use the Save As command to save an existing file in a different location or format under a different name.

Digital rodent replacement

Ctrl+S

Ribbon bar icon

Using Save & Save As

1. Choose Save (or Save As) from the File menu.
2. If you choose Save and the image already has a name, Photo-Paint saves the image to disk.

176 Save... (Save Transparency Mask)

3. If this is the first time you have saved the image or you select Save As, the Save an Image to Disk dialog box opens.

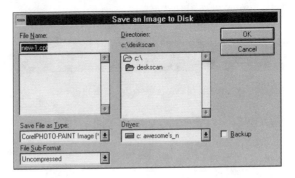

4. Name the file and select the Drive and Directory in which you want to store it.
5. If you want to save it in another format, select that format from the drop-down list.
6. Click on OK.

Save... (Save Transparency Mask)

Saves a mask or a transparency mask to disk so it can be used again.

Using Mask⇨Save

1. Create the mask that you want to save.
2. Choose Save or Save Transparency Mask from the Mask menu to open the Save an Image to Disk dialog box.
3. Give the file a Name and select a Drive and Directory in which to store it.
4. If you want to save it in another format, choose that format from the Save File as Type drop-down list.
5. Click on OK.

Select Partial Area...

Screen Dithering

- ⇨ Error Diffusion
- ⇨ Ordered

If you are stuck with a monitor/video card combination that cannot display more than 256 colors, but you still need to use a program as demanding as Photo-Paint, you can use this command to get a more attractive look on your monitor.

Using Screen Dithering

Choose Screen Dithering from the View menu. From the flyout menu, choose Error diffusion for the best — but slowest — results, or choose Ordered for quicker redraws but less attractive displays.

More stuff

The Screen Dithering command is not available if you are using a driver capable of the displaying more than 256 colors.

Select

Only one of the four tool modes listed in the Special menu can be active at a time. The four modes are Select, Add To Selection, Remove From Selection, and XOR Selection. When the Select command is active, objects and masks created with tools become defined areas.

Ribbon bar icon

Using Select

To make the selection mode active, choose Special⇨Select.

Select Partial Area...

If only part of an image is open for modification, you can use the Select Partial Area command to open another segment of the same image.

178 Sharpen

Using Select Partial Area

To open another part of an image:

1. Choose Select Partial Area from the File menu. The image opens in the Partial Area dialog box, showing the same grid pattern that you used to open the image part in the Open an Image dialog box.

2. To select another portion of the image while maintaining the same grid pattern, click on the grid square that you want to open.
3. Click on OK.

More stuff

If you want to resize the grid, choose a grid size from the drop-down list or click on the Edit Grid checkbox to create a grid by dragging the gridlines.

Sharpen

See Effects & Filters.

Skew

To precisely skew an object, follow these steps:

Split Channels To

1. Select the object that you want to squish.
2. Choose S<u>k</u>ew from the <u>O</u>bject menu.
3. Click on the Skew button in the Tool Settings roll-up if it is not already active.
4. Enter the amount of skew you want in the H and V boxes.

You can do this procedure with the mouse, too. Double-click on the object until the rotation arrows appear and then drag one of the four side handles to skew the object. Check out the status line while you're skewing to see the skew angle, which gives you a pretty good guidepost.

5. Click on Apply to apply the skew to the object, or click on Apply To Duplicate to create a new object with the specified skew.

Soften

See Effe<u>c</u>ts & Filters.

Special

See Effe<u>c</u>ts & Filters.

<u>S</u>plit Channels To

- ⇨ <u>R</u>GB
- ⇨ <u>C</u>YMK
- ⇨ <u>H</u>SB
- ⇨ HL<u>S</u>
- ⇨ <u>Y</u>IQ

Creates a gray-scale image of each color channel. Allows you to edit one or more color channels without changing the others.

Using <u>S</u>plit Channels To

1. Choose <u>S</u>plit Channels To from the <u>I</u>mage menu.
2. Select the color model that you want to use for the split:

180 Stretch

- **RGB:** Red, green, blue
- **CMYK:** Cyan, magenta, yellow, black
- **HSBV:** Hue, saturation, brightness value
- **HLS:** Hue, lightness, saturation
- **YIQ:** Luminance, chromaticity

Stretch

To precisely stretch an object, follow these steps:

1. Select the object that you want to stretch.
2. Choose Stretch from the Object menu.
3. Click on the Size button if it is not already active.
4. Enter the new measurements in the H and V boxes.

You can do this procedure with the mouse. Click on the object until the selection handles appear and then either drag the corner handles to scale the object or drag the side handles to stretch it. Check out the status line while you're dragging or scaling. The percentage of change appears, giving you a pretty good guidepost.

5. Click on Apply to apply the size to the object, or click on Apply To Duplicate to create a new object with the specified size.

Tile Horizontally, Tile Vertically

Unlike Draw, Photo-Paint allows you to open several images at the same time. To avoid being sent to bed without your supper because of slovenly screen habits, you may want to tile all your pictures neatly, one right next to the other. The Tile commands do so automatically, saving you much frustration.

Digital rodent replacement

Shift+F4 for Tile Vertically

Using Tile

If you have a deep-seated need to be neat or a disapproving significant other, choose Tile Horizontally or Tile Vertically from the Windows menu to display all your open pictures tidily ordered.

Tool Settings Roll-Up 181

Tone

 See Eff<u>e</u>cts & Filters.

Tool Settings Roll-Up

Adjusts the aspects, shape, and other factors of the tool that is selected.

Digital rodent replacement
Ctrl+F8

Using the Tool Settings roll-up

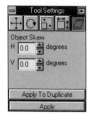

- ✔ Selecting Tool Settings when the Object Picker tool is active opens the dialog box that I discuss under the Distort command.

- ✔ Selecting Tool Settings when the Eyedropper tool is active opens a dialog box that allows you to change the area that the tool uses to select a color.

- ✔ Selecting Tool Settings when the Local Undo tool is active opens a dialog box that allows you to change the size and shape of the brush.

- ✔ Selecting Tool Settings when the Line tool is active opens a dialog box that allows you to change the size and shape of the brush and modify the transparency and spacing of the lines.

- ✔ Selecting Tool Settings when the Paintbrush tool is active opens a dialog box that allows you to change the size and shape of the brush and modify the transparency, spacing, density, and fadeout of the lines and the sharpness of the edges of the brushstrokes.

Toolbox

- ✔ Selecting Tool Settings when the Rectangle tool is active opens a dialog box that allows you to adjust the roundness of the corners of a rectangle.
- ✔ Selecting Tool Settings when the Fill tool is active allows you to set color tolerance.
- ✔ Selecting Tool Settings when the Smear tool is active opens a dialog box that allows you to change the size and shape of the brush and modify the transparency, spacing, density, and fadeout of the lines and the sharpness of the edges of the brushstrokes.
- ✔ Selecting Tool Settings when the Clone tool is active opens a dialog box that allows you to change the size and shape of the brush and modify the transparency, spacing, density, and fadeout of the lines and the sharpness of the edges of the brushstrokes.

Toolbox

 ➪ Visible
 ➪ Floating

Lets you see the toolbox, or not see the toolbox, in two attractive versions and in a location of your choice.

Digital rodent replacement

Ctrl+T toggles tools between visible and invisible.

Using Toolbox

To hide or show the toolbox, choose Visible from the Toolbox flyout in the View menu.

If you want the toolbox to float so that you can reposition it wherever you want, choose Floating from the Toolbox flyout in the View menu.

More stuff

If you want to see all the Photo-Paint tools in one big block, do the following:

1. Choose Floating from the Toolbox flyout in the View menu.
2. Choose Grouped from the Control menu of the floating toolbox. (The Control menu looks like a spacebar or a dash in the upper-left corner of the box.) The result is as follows:

XOR Selection

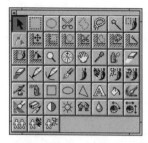

Transformations

See Effe*c*ts & Filters.

*U*ndo

Reverses the actions that you performed since you last chose a tool or issued a command. The *U*ndo command name changes as you perform actions.

Digital rodent replacement

Ctrl+Z

*Using U*ndo

Choose *U*ndo from the *E*dit menu.

*X*OR Selection

Only one of the four tool modes listed in the Special menu can be active at a time. The four modes are S*e*lect, *A*dd To Selection, *R*emove From Selection, and *X*OR Selection. When *X*OR Selection is active, any areas that do not overlap in objects and masks created with tools are eliminated from the defined area.

Ribbon bar icon

Using XOR Selection

To activate XOR selection mode, choose Special⇨XOR Selection.

More stuff

If masks or objects are defined with XOR Selection active and do not share any areas, all areas are combined and can be manipulated as if they were one.

Zoom

Lets you zoom in on an image at magnification levels you choose from the flyout menu.

Using Zoom

Choose View⇨Zoom and then choose the level of magnification you want from the flyout menu.

Zoom		25%
100% (No Zoom)	Ctrl+1	33%
Zoom To Fit	F4	50%
Rulers	Ctrl+R	200%
Toolbox		300%
Color Roll-Up	Ctrl+F2	400%
Canvas Roll-Up	Ctrl+F3	600%
Fill Roll-Up	Shift+F6	1600%
Tool Settings Roll-Up	Ctrl+F8	
Screen Dithering	▶	
Color Correction	▶	
Maximize Work Area		
Full-Screen Preview	F9	

Zoom To Fit

Automatically zooms in or out to make the image fit on the desktop.

Digital rodent replacement

F4

Using Zoom To Fit

Choose Zoom To Fit from the View menu.

Object Picker Tools 185

More stuff

Using Zoom To Fit is a useful way to get back to a global view of your image after you zoom in on a part of it.

The Part of Tools and Other Neato Stuff

If you thought CorelDraw had a lot of tools, you ain't seen nuttin' yet! Photo-Paint has 53 different tools, some more useful than others. Unfortunately, there are few shortcuts, and some tools don't work quite the same way as they do in Draw. It does keep life challenging, though.

Many of these tools are discussed in detail in Chapter 15 of *CorelDRAW! 5 For Dummies*.

Object Picker Tools

Clicking and holding the left mouse button while pointing to the Object Picker tool opens the object-picking, creating, and shape-changing flyout menu. It contains the tools in the following table:

Tool	What It Does
▶	Use the Object Picker tool to choose or size an object after you create it with one of the Object Creating tools.
▢	Creates rectangular objects.
○	Creates circular (or oval) objects.
✂	Creates polygonal objects. Click once to anchor the first node and then click at each subsequent node point. Double-click to close the polygon.
◌	Creates irregularly shaped objects. Drag the mouse to draw the object. Releasing the mouse button closes the shape.
⌕	Creates an irregular object from image areas with similar colors.

(continued)

Mask Picker Tools

Tool	What It Does
	Creates an object over an area of similar color, but excludes the background. Use the Color Tolerance dialog box in the Special menu to set the color selection tolerance.
	Creates an object composed of brushstrokes.
	Use this tool when in Build Mode to edit the nodes of build objects.

Shortcuts

Double-clicking on the Object Picker tool (the first tool) opens the Objects/Layers roll-up.

Double-clicking on the Create Irregular Object tool (the fifth tool) opens the Color Tolerance roll-up.

Double-clicking on the lasso opens the Color Tolerance roll-up.

Double-clicking on the magic wand opens the Color Tolerance roll-up.

Double-clicking on the brush opens the Color Tolerance roll-up.

Double-clicking on the Node Edit tool (the last tool) opens the Tool Settings/Precision roll-up.

Mask Picker Tools

Clicking the left mouse button while pointing to the Mask Picker (what Black Bart wanted to be to the Lone Ranger) tool opens the mask-picking, creating, and shape-changing flyout menu. It contains the following tools.

Tool	What It Does
	Use the Mask Picker tool to choose or size a mask after you create it with one of the Mask Creating tools.
	Creates rectangular masks.
	Creates circular (or oval) masks.
	Creates polygonal masks. Click once to anchor the first node and then click at each subsequent node point. Double-click to close the polygon.

Zoom Tools

Tool	What It Does
	Creates irregularly shaped masks. Drag the mouse to draw the object, and release the mouse button to close the shape.
	Creates an irregular mask over images with similar colors.
	Creates a mask over an area of similar color, exclusive of the background. You can set the color selection tolerance in the Color Tolerance dialog box in the Special menu.
	Creates a mask composed of brushstrokes.
	Node-edits a mask that you created with any of the Mask Creation tools.

Shortcuts

Double-clicking on the Mask Picker tool (the first tool) opens the Objects/Layers roll-up.

Double-clicking on a Rectangular, Circular, or Polygonal Mask tool (the second, third, and fourth tools) adds a frame mask (outside mask) to the shape mask created.

Double-clicking on the Create Irregular Mask tool (the fifth tool) opens the Color Tolerance roll-up.

Double-clicking on the lasso opens the Color Tolerance roll-up.

Double-clicking on the magic wand opens the Color Tolerance roll-up.

Double-clicking on the brush opens the Color Tolerance roll-up.

Double-clicking on the Node Edit tool (the last tool) opens the Tool Settings/Precision roll-up.

Zoom Tools

Use these tools to get up close and personal or to maintain your distance to your image.

Undo Tools

Tool	What It Does
🔍	Select this tool, point to an area of your image, and then click the left mouse button to zoom in or the right button to zoom out. You can also marquee-select an area to zoom in on.
⊕	Helps poor little lambs find their way. Shows you where you are in one window when you're viewing the same image in another, usually at greatly increased magnification.
✋	Moves a magnified image about in the current window to get a better look at it. Does not come with cloven hooves, horns, or pipe.
💧	Selects a color from the image. Point to the color and click the left mouse button to make it the paint color or the right mouse button to make it the fill color.

Shortcut

Double-click on the Eyedropper tool to open the Color roll-up.

Undo Tools

These tools provide you with three different flavors of erasers.

Tool	What It Does
	Undoes that which you last did in the area you define with the brush supplied by this tool. (Open the Tool Settings roll-up to change the brush size and shape.)
	Erases the image under the eraser brush. (Open the Tool Settings roll-up to change the brush size and shape.)
	Replaces the currently selected paint color with the paper color.

Paint Brush Tools

Line Tools

These tools draw lines.

Tool	What It Does
	Draws 'em straight.
	Draws 'em curved.
	Draws 'em freehand.

Shortcut

Double-clicking on any Line tool opens the Tool Settings roll-up for line and brush shapes.

Paint Brush Tools

Use these tools to create brushstrokes or to spray or splatter color with great discrimination.

Tool	What It Does
	Works just like a real paintbrush.
	Creates a brushstroke composed of lines of varying shades of the paint color.
	Creates a brushstroke composed of dots of varying shades of the paint color.
	Creates a brushstroke from a saved brush style.
	Sprays the paint color with much abandon, but is still constrained by the brush shape.
	Splatters the paint color within the confines of the brush shape.

190 Shape Tools

Shortcuts

Double-clicking on the Paintbrush tool opens the Brush Shapes roll-up.

Double-clicking on the Impressionism Brush tool (the second tool) opens the Impressionism roll-up.

Double-clicking on the Pointillism Brush tool (the third tool) opens the Pointillism roll-up.

Double clicking on the Artist Brush tool (the fourth tool) opens the Tool Settings roll-up and lets you choose a saved brush style.

Double-clicking on the Spray tool opens the Brush Shapes roll-up.

Double-clicking on the Splatter tool opens the Brush Shapes roll-up.

Shape Tools

These tools create geometric shapes that assume the current fill and paint colors.

Tool	What It Does
□	Draws squares and rectangles.
○	Draws circles and ovals.
△	Draws polygons. Click once to anchor the first node and then click on each subsequent node location. Double-click to close the shape.

Shortcuts

Double-clicking on the Square tool opens the Tool Settings roll-up, which allows you to adjust line size and corner rounding.

Double-clicking on the Circle tool opens the Tool Settings roll-up, which allows you to adjust line size and transparency.

Double-clicking on the Polygon tool opens the Tool Settings roll-up, which allows you to adjust line size, type of joint, and transparency.

Text Tool

Inserts text at the cursor location. Click the I-beam cursor where you want the text to appear.

Shortcut

Double-clicking on the Text tool opens the Font dialog box, where you can change your font, style, size, and other text attributes.

Fill Tool

Applies a fill to objects.

Shortcut

Double-clicking on the Fill tool opens the Fill roll-up.

Smear, Smudge, Contrast, Brightness, and Color Tools

Here, Corel stuck all the tools that it really didn't know where else to put.

Tool	What It Does
	Smears two or more colors together, much like finger-painting.
	Smudges the colors together. It's not nearly as satisfying as the Smear tool.
	Sharpens the image where the brush shape passes over it.

(continued)

Clone Tools

Tool	What It Does
◐	Increases or decreases contrast in the area painted by the brush shape.
☼	Lightens or darkens the portion of the image where the brush shape passes over it.
🎨	Applies a tint of the paint color to the image.
◊	Softly blends the colors under the cursor.
🎡	Adjusts the amount and type of color (hue).
🔧	Adjusts the amount of color saturation.

Shortcuts

Double-clicking on any of these tools opens the Tool Settings roll-up specific to that tool.

Clone Tools

These tools make copies of areas of the image and place them elsewhere on the image. They're useful for taking background clutter out of a photograph or removing unsightly moles from the faces of models.

Tool	What It Does
👥	Paints an area identical to the original. Position the cursor on the part of the image you want to copy and click once; then position the cursor at the place to which you want to copy and paint the copy in place. Click the right mouse button to start again with new tool positions.
👥	Paints a copy of the original that looks almost nothing like it and applies the impressionist brush. Use it like the real Clone tool.
👥	Paints a copy of the original that looks even less like it. It applies the pointillism brush. You use it the same way you use the real Clone tool.

Index

• A •

Acquire Image (CorelPhoto-Paint File menu), 124–125
Add Perspective (CorelDraw Effects menu), 5–6
Add To Selection (CorelPhoto-Paint Special menu), 125–126
Adobe Illustrator
 file format for exports to, 36
 file format for imports from, 47
AI extensions, 36, 47
Align... (CorelDraw Arrange menu), 6–7
aligning
 objects, 6–7
 text, 103
 text to baseline, 7–8
Align to Baseline (CorelDraw Text menu), 7–8
All (CorelPhoto-Paint Mask menu), 126
All (CorelPhoto-Paint Object menu), 126
Alt+key combinations in CorelDraw
 Alt+Enter for Redo, 87
 Alt+F1 for Mosaic Roll-Up, 56–58
 Alt+F2 for font access with Dimension lines pencil tool, 119
 Alt+F3 for Lens Roll-Up, 52–54
 Alt+F4 for Exit, 34–35
 Alt+F5 for Presets Roll-Up, 80–81
 Alt+F7 for Transform Roll-Ups, 106–110
 Alt+F10 for Align to Baseline, 7
Alt+key combinations in CorelPhoto-Paint
 Alt+F1 for Mosaic Roll-Up, 161–162
 Alt+F4 for Exit, 150–151
Ami Professional file format for exports, 36
applications
 OLE links to/from, 54–55
 opening other programs to create objects to link, 49
Apply Style (CorelDraw Object menu), 8–9
archive of available files, 56–58
arcs, 33–34
Arrange Icons (CorelPhoto-Paint Windows menu), 126–127
Arrange menu of CorelDraw
 Align..., 6–7
 Break Apart, 13
 Combine, 21
 Convert To Curves, 23–24
 Group, 44–45
 Intersection, 50–51
 Order, 63–64
 Separate, 96–97
 Trim, 110
 Ungroup, 114
 Weld, 114–115
arrows, creating with Callout tool, 119
arrow shapes, creating, 27
Artistic filter (CorelPhoto-Paint Effects menu), 151
Artistic text, 9
 changing default text attributes for, 14
 editing, 32–33
 merging, 86
 spell checking, 98–99
 types of styles for, 94, 101
Arts & Letters
 file format for exports to, 36
 file format for imports from, 47
ASCII text files
 importing, 47
 saving text objects as, 36–37
attributes
 copying, 26–27
 saving as styles, 93–94
 selecting, 103
AutoCAD
 file format for exports to, 36
 file format for imports from, 47
AutoJoin, setting preferences for, 77

automatic text string replacement, 112
AutoReduce, setting preferences for, 77
Autotracing
  easing with hidden bitmaps, 10
  setting preferences for, 77

• B •

backgrounds
  applying in CorelPhoto-Paint, 128–129
  choosing colors in CorelPhoto-Paint, 138
  excluding from objects in CorelPhoto-Paint, 186
backups
  importance of, 80
  setting preferences for automatic, 79
baselines
  aligning text by, 7–8
  fitting to graphic object's outline, 40–41
  restoring text to, 99–100
Bezier tool, 119
bitmaps
  cropping or resampling in CorelPhoto-Paint, 129
  cropping with Shape tool in CorelDraw, 117
  fills in CorelPhoto-Paint, 155
  hiding in CorelDraw, 9
  importing into CorelDraw, 47–48
  importing into CorelPhoto-Paint, 128–129
  reducing screen redraw time in CorelDraw, 9
Bitmaps (CorelDraw View menu), 9–10
Blend Roll-Up, 10–13
blends
  cloning, 16
  constructing, 11–12
  copying, 24–25
  separating original from intermediate objects, 96
  specifying anchor nodes for special effects, 12
  splitting, 12–13
BMP files
  format for imports into CorelDraw, 47
  importing for colors in CorelPhoto-Paint, 140
Break Apart (CorelDraw Arrange menu), 13
brightness of images in CorelPhoto-Paint, 131–132
brushstroke tool in CorelPhoto-Paint, 186
Build Mode (CorelPhoto-Paint Object menu), 127–128
bullets, 69–70

• C •

calibration bar for colors
  in CorelDraw, 84
  in CorelPhoto-Paint, 169
calligraphic pen outlines, 79
Callout tool, 119
canvases
  embossing in CorelPhoto-Paint, 129
  importing into CorelPhoto-Paint, 128–129
Canvas Roll-Up (CorelPhoto-Paint View menu), 128–129
capitalization assistance, 111
Cascade (CorelPhoto-Paint Windows menu), 129–130
case matching in find-and-replace operations, 89
CDR extensions, 47
center alignment tabs, 68
centering text, 67
centimeters, 44
CGM extensions, 36
channels for colors in CorelPhoto-Paint
  combining, 141
  creating gray-scale images of, 179–180
Character... (CorelDraw Text menu), 13–14
character spacing, 67
Checkpoint (CorelPhoto-Paint Edit menu), 130
checkpoints in CorelPhoto-Paint
  marking, 130
  restoring images to point before changes, 173
circles
  creating arcs and wedges with CorelDraw Shape tool, 117
  drawing with CorelPhoto-Paint circle/oval tool, 185
Circle tool in CorelPhoto-Paint, 190
Clear (CorelDraw Effects menu), 15
Clear (CorelPhoto-Paint Edit menu), 130–131
Clear Transformations (CorelDraw Effects menu), 15
Clipboard, 70–71

See also Paste *commands*; pasting
Clone (CorelDraw Edit menu), 15–16
Clone (CorelDraw Effects menu), 16–17
clones
  of objects, 15–16
  reverting to master, 90
  selecting, 96
  separating original from intermediate objects, 96
  setting preferences for placement of, 75
  of special effects, 16–17
Clone tools in CorelPhoto-Paint, 192
Close (CorelPhoto-Paint File menu), 131
CMX extensions, 36
Color (CorelPhoto-Paint Effects menu), 131–134
Color Correction (CorelDraw View menu), 17
Color Correction (CorelPhoto-Paint View menu), 134–135
color format conversion in CorelPhoto-Paint, 141–142
Color Manager... (CorelDraw File menu), 18–19
Color Manager... (CorelPhoto-Paint File menu), 135–137
Color Mask Roll-Up (CorelPhoto-Paint Mask menu), 137–138
color-matching systems, 20
Color Palette (CorelDraw View menu), 19–21
Color Roll-Up (CorelPhoto-Paint View menu), 138–140
colors
  adding, brightening or inverting with lens, 53
  adjustment tools of CorelPhoto-Paint, 192
  for blends, 12
  choosing in CorelPhoto-Paint, 138
  customized, 20
  for custom patterns, 28–29
  for extrudes, 38
  finding names of, 21
  with Outline Pen tool, 121
  overprinting for traps, 64–65
  for paper, 66
  preferences for dithering scheme, 80
  printing calibration bar, 84, 169
  profiling (System Color Profile), 17, 18–19, 134–137
  selecting in CorelPhoto-Paint, 153–156
  selecting ranges for CorelPhoto-Paint Magic Wand or Fill tool, 140–141
  separations in, 85, 170
Color Tolerance (CorelPhoto-Paint Special menu), 140–141
columns for Paragraph text, 41–42
Combine Channels (CorelPhoto-Paint Image menu), 141
Combine (CorelDraw Arrange menu), 21
commands
  redoing, 87
  repeating, 88
  undoing, 112–113
complex objects in CorelPhoto-Paint
  adding new areas to, 125
  combining several areas into one, 127–128
  removing areas from, 172
  selecting entire, 126
concentric objects, 22
Contents (CorelDraw Help menu), 22
Contour Roll-Up (CorelDraw Effects menu), 22–23
contours, separating original from intermediate objects, 96
contrast tool of CorelPhoto-Paint, 192
Convert To (CorelPhoto-Paint Image menu), 141–142
Convert To Curves (CorelDraw Arrange menu), 23–24
Copy Attributes From... (CorelDraw Edit menu), 26–27
Copy (CorelDraw Edit menu), 25–26
Copy (CorelDraw Effects menu), 24–25
Copy (CorelPhoto-Paint Edit menu), 142–143
copying
  attributes, 26–27
  objects, 25–26
  objects in CorelPhoto-Paint, 142–143, 150
  special effects, 24–25
Copy To File (CorelPhoto-Paint Edit menu), 143
CorelDraw
  exiting, 34–35
  file format for imports from, 47
  tutorial, 110–111
Corel Image Source, 124
CorelPhoto-Paint, changes in version E1, 123
CorelTrace file format for imports, 47

CorelVentura file format for exports, 36
CPT file format for imports, 47
Create Arrow... (CorelDraw Special menu), 27–28
Create Brush (CorelPhoto-Paint Special menu), 144–145
Create (CorelPhoto-Paint Object menu), 143–144
Create Pattern... (CorelDraw Special menu), 28–29
Create Symbol... (CorelDraw Special menu), 29–30
Create Transparency Mask (CorelPhoto-Paint Mask menu), 145–146
Crop Image (CorelPhoto-Paint Mask menu), 146–147
crop marks, 84, 169
cropping
  bitmaps in CorelDraw with Shape tool, 117
  images in CorelPhoto-Paint, 146–147
cross-hair style mouse pointer, 77
Ctrl+key combinations in CorelDraw
  Ctrl+A for Align, 6–7
  Ctrl+B for Blend Roll-Up, 10–13
  Ctrl+C for Copy, 25–26
  Ctrl+D for Duplicate, 32
  Ctrl+E for Extrude Roll-Up, 37–39
  Ctrl+F for Fit Text To Path, 40–41
  Ctrl+F1 for Search For Help On, 94–95
  Ctrl+F2 for Paragraph..., 66–70
  Ctrl+F2 for Text Roll-Up, 103–104
  Ctrl+F3 for Layers Roll-Up, 51–52
  Ctrl+F5 for Apply Style, 8
  Ctrl+F5 for Styles Roll-Up, 100–101
  Ctrl+F7 for Envelope Roll-Up, 33–34
  Ctrl+F8 for PowerLine Roll-Up, 73–75
  Ctrl+F9 for Contour Roll-Up, 22–23
  Ctrl+F11 for Symbols Roll-Up, 101–102
  Ctrl+G for Group, 44–45
  Ctrl+J for Preferences..., 75–80
  Ctrl+K for Break Apart, 13
  Ctrl+L for Combine, 21
  Ctrl+N for New, 58
  Ctrl+O for Open..., 62–63
  Ctrl+P for Print..., 82–85
  Ctrl+PgUp/PgDn keys for rearranging stacking order of objects, 63–64
  Ctrl+Q for Convert To Curves, 23–24
  Ctrl+R for Repeat, 88
  Ctrl+S for saving, 80, 92–93
  Ctrl+Shift+T for Edit Text..., 32–33
  Ctrl+T for Character..., 13–14
  Ctrl+U for Ungroup, 114
  Ctrl+V for Paste, 70–71
  Ctrl+W for Refresh Window, 87–88
  Ctrl+X for Cut, 30–31
  Ctrl+Z for Undo (CorelDraw Edit menu), 76, 112–113
  preferences for constrain angle with, 76
Ctrl+key combinations in CorelPhoto-Paint
  Ctrl+1 for "unzooming," 124
  Ctrl+C for Copy, 142–143
  Ctrl+D for Duplicate, 150
  Ctrl+F7 for Layers/Objects Roll-Up, 158–159
  Ctrl+F8 for CorelPhoto-Paint Tool Settings Roll-Up, 181–182
  Ctrl+G for Merge, 160–161
  Ctrl+J for Preferences, 166–167
  Ctrl+N for New, 162–163
  Ctrl+O for Open, 163–164
  Ctrl+P for Print..., 167–170
  Ctrl+S for Save, 175–176
  Ctrl+T for toggling tools between visible and invisible, 182–183
  Ctrl+V for Paste, 165
  Ctrl+X for Cut, 147
  Ctrl+Z for Undo, 183
curves
  adjusting with Shape tool, 117
  with Bezier tool, 119
  changing to/from lines, 60
  drawing tools in CorelPhoto-Paint, 189
  setting preferences for accuracy of tracking/drawing, 77–78
cusp nodes, 60
Cut (CorelDraw Edit menu), 30–31
Cut (CorelPhoto-Paint Edit menu), 147

• D •

days, capitalizing names of, 111
DDE applications, 54, 55
decimal tabs, 68
Delete (CorelDraw Edit menu), 31
Delete (CorelPhoto-Paint Object menu), 147
Delete key
  for Clear (in CorelPhoto-Paint), 130–131

for Delete (in CorelPhoto-Paint), 147
Delete Page... (CorelDraw Layout menu), 31
deleting
  fills, 122
  masks in CorelPhoto-Paint, 130–131
  masks or objects in CorelPhoto-Paint, 130–131
  pages, 31
  paths of fitted text, 41
Delrina Perform file format for exports, 36
densitometer scale
  in CorelDraw, 84
  in CorelPhoto-Paint, 169
dictionaries for spell checking, 99
Distort (CorelPhoto-Paint Object menu), 148–150
dithering in CorelPhoto-Paint, 177
documents
  printing in CorelPhoto-Paint, 167–170
  See also drawings
drawing areas in CorelPhoto-Paint, opening new, 162–163
drawings
  assigning elements to different layers, 51–52
  clearing old and creating new, 58
  creating from templates, 58–59
  full-screen views of, 42–43
  loading into CorelPhoto-Paint, 163–164
  naming, 92
  positioning at print time, 84
Duplicate (CorelDraw Edit menu), 32
Duplicate (CorelPhoto-Paint Object menu), 150
DXF extensions, 36, 47

• E •

Edit menu of CorelDraw
  Clone, 15–16
  Copy, 25–26
  Copy Attributes From..., 26–27
  Cut, 30–31
  Delete, 31
  Duplicate, 32
  Insert Object..., 48–49
  Links..., 54–55
  New From Template..., 58–59
  Paste, 70–71
  Paste Special..., 71–72
  Redo, 87
  Repeat, 88
  Select All, 95
  Undo, 76, 112–113
Edit menu of CorelPhoto-Paint
  Checkpoint, 130
  Clear, 130–131
  Copy, 142–143
  Copy To File, 143
  Cut, 147
  Font, 156
  Paste, 165
  Paste From File, 166
  Restore To Checkpoint, 173
  Undo, 183
Edit Text... (CorelDraw Text menu), 32–33
Effects menu of CorelDraw
  Add Perspective, 5–6
  Clear, 15
  Clear Transformations, 15
  Clone, 16–17
  Contour Roll-Up, 22–23
  Copy, 24–25
  Envelope Roll-Up, 33–34
  Extrude Roll-Up, 37–39
  Lens Roll-Up, 52–54
  PowerClip, 72–73
  PowerLine Roll-Up, 73–75
  Transform Roll-Ups, 106–110
Effects menu of CorelPhoto-Paint
  Artistic filter, 151
  Color, 131–134
  Fancy filter, 151
  Mapping filter, 152
  Noise filter, 152
  Sharpen filter, 152–153
  Soften filter, 153
  Special filter, 153
  Tone filter, 153
  Transformations filter, 153
ellipses
  converting to curves, 23–24
  creating arcs and wedges with Shape tool, 117
  creating with Ellipse tool, 119–120
Ellipse tool (CorelDraw Tools menu), 119–120
embedding objects, 48–49
embossing canvases in CorelPhoto-Paint, 129
emulsion side down, 84, 169
envelope effects, resetting, 15
Envelope Roll-Up (CorelDraw Effects menu), 33–34
EPS extensions, 36, 47
EPS format for file exports, 36

erasers (Undo tools in CorelPhoto-Paint), 188
Excel (Graphs) file format for imports, 47
Exit (CorelDraw File menu), 34–35
Exit (CorelPhoto-Paint File menu), 150–151
Export... (CorelDraw File menu), 35–36
exporting
  files, 35–36
  text with attributes or as curves, 79
extensions
  file formats for imports, 36
  recommended file formats for exports, 36
Extract... (CorelDraw Special menu), 36–37
extracted objects
  returning to current drawing, 56
  saving as ASCII files, 36–37
Extrude Roll-Up (CorelDraw Effects menu), 37–39
extrudes
  separating original from intermediate objects, 96
  setting preferences for minimum facet size, 77

• F •

facing pages, 66
Fancy filter (CorelPhoto-Paint Effects menu), 151
feet as unit of measurement, 44
file formats recommended for non-PostScript printers, 36
File menu of CorelDraw
  Color Manager..., 18–19
  Exit, 34–35
  Export..., 35–36
  Import..., 46–48
  Mosaic Roll-Up..., 56–58
  New, 58
  Open..., 62–63
  Print..., 82–85
  Print Merge..., 86
  Print Setup..., 86–87
  Save, 92–93
File menu of CorelPhoto-Paint
  Acquire Image, 124–125
  Close, 131
  Color Manager..., 135–137
  Exit, 150–151
  Mosaic Roll-Up, 161–162
  New, 162–163
  Open, 163–164
  Print..., 167–170
  Print Setup..., 170–171
  Save, 175–176
  Save As..., 175–176
  Select Partial Area..., 177–178
filename extensions. See extensions
files
  visual archive of CorelDraw's available, 56–58
  visual archive of CorelPhoto-Paint's available, 161–162
file transfers (exports), 35–36
Fill Roll-Up (CorelPhoto-Paint View menu), 153–156
Fill tool in CorelPhoto-Paint, 140, 191
Fill tools (CorelDraw Tools menu), 121–122
Find... (CorelDraw Text menu), 39–40
finding
  drawings using keywords, 63
  "lost" objects, 26, 95
  and replacing text, 88–89
  text, 39–40
Fit Text To Path (CorelDraw Text menu), 40–41
Flip (CorelPhoto-Paint Object menu), 156
floating toolbox, 105
FOCOLTONE color-matching system, 20
Font (CorelPhoto-Paint Edit menu), 156
font matching preferences, 79
fonts
  preferences for display of samples of, 78
  selecting in CorelDraw, 103
  selecting in CorelPhoto-Paint, 156
  Type 1, 85
fountain fills
  with CorelDraw Fill tool, 121
  with CorelPhoto-Paint Fill tool, 154–155
  preference settings for, 77
  steps or bands in, 85
Frame... (CorelDraw Text menu), 41–42
frames
  applying formatting to, 104
  dragging for Paragraph text placement, 120
  for pages, 66
Freehand mode, setting preferences for tracking, 77–78
Freehand tool, 119

Index

Full-Screen Preview (CorelDraw View menu), 42–43
   viewing all or only selected objects in, 82
Full-Screen Preview (CorelPhoto-Paint View menu), 157
Function keys in CorelDraw
   F1 for help, 22
   F2 for Zoom In tool, 118
   F3 for Canvas Roll-Up (CorelPhoto-Paint), 128–129
   F3 for Zoom Out tool, 118
   F3 to return to preceding view, 118
   F4 for bringing all objects into view, 118
   F6 for Rectangle tool, 119
   F7 for Ellipse tool, 120
   F8 for Artistic text tool, 120
   F9 for Full-Screen Preview, 42–43
   F10 for Shape tool, 117
   F12 for Outline Pen, 120–121
Function keys in CorelPhoto-Paint
   F2 for Color Roll-Up, 138–140
   F4 for Color Mask Roll-Up, 137–138
   F4 for Zoom To Fit, 184–185

• G •

Gamma value of images in CorelPhoto-Paint, 132
GEM Artline
   file format for exports to, 36
   file format for imports from, 47
GEM Draw Plus file format for imports, 48
GEM extensions, 36, 47
GEM Graph file format for imports, 48
GIF file format for imports, 47
graphics
   embedding or linking, 48
   precise positioning of, 106–110
Graphic text, 9
   types of styles for, 94, 101
gray-scale images in CorelPhoto-Paint, 179–180
greeking of text, 78–79
Grid & Scale Setup... (CorelDraw Layout menu), 43–44
grid
   showing, 44, 97
   snapping objects to, 44, 97
Group (CorelDraw Arrange menu), 44–45
groups
   clearing transformations from, 15
   nested, 45
   of objects, 44–45
guidelines
   adjusting, 45
   for precise alignment of objects, 45
   snapping to, 98
Guidelines Setup... (CorelDraw Layout menu), 45–46
gutters, manual calculations for, 42

• H •

halftone separations, 85, 169
"hand" cursor in CorelPhoto-Paint, 151
hanging indents, 69
Harvard Graphics file format for imports, 48
heatmaps, 53
help (F1), 22
Help menu of CorelDraw
   Contents, 22
   Screen/Menu Help..., 94
   Search For Help On, 94–95
   Tutorial, 110–111
hiding
   bitmaps, 9
   gridlines, 44
   ribbon bar, status line, pop-up help messages, 77
   rulers, 92, 175
   toolbox, 105
High resolution, 9
horizontal alignment, 7
   to gridlines, 44
   with guidelines, 45
   with tabs, 68
hotkeys for styles, 101
Hot Zone for automatic hyphenation, 67
hue of images in CorelPhoto-Paint, adjusting, 133
hyphenation, automatic, 67

• I •

icons
   for active roll-ups, 91
   of grouped floating toolbox, 105
   for printer's marks, 84
   as used in this book, 1–3
   See also individual commands; tools
icons in CorelPhoto-Paint
   arranging minimized, 126
   See also tools in CorelPhoto-Paint
Image menu of CorelPhoto-Paint
   Combine Channels, 141

Convert To, 141–142
Info..., 157
Paper Size, 164–165
Resample..., 172–173
Rotate, 174–175
Split Channels To, 179–180
images in CorelPhoto-Paint
　adjusting color brightness, contrast, Gamma value, hue, saturation and tone maps, 131–134
　adjusting size or resolution, 172–173
　applying masks to, 126
　arranging as minimized icons, 126
　cascading for neatened screen, 129–130
　cloning areas of, 192
　closing, 131
　converting to other color formats, 141–142
　cropping, 146–147
　displaying information about, 157
　editing and positioning, 158–159
　filters and special effects for, 151–153
　flipping, 156
　gray-scale for each color channel, 179–180
　opening another segment of, 177–178
　pasting from Clipboard, 165
　pasting from files, 166
　pulling into CorelPhoto-Paint, 124–125
　rotating, 174–175
　saving at checkpoints like bookmarks, 130
　tiling, 180
Import... (CorelDraw File menu), 46–48
importing
　BMP files for colors in CorelPhoto-Paint, 140
　canvases into CorelPhoto-Paint, 128–129
　drawings and automatic page additions to accommodate, 50
　drawings into CorelDraw, 46–48
inches as unit of measurement, 14, 44, 46
indention
　of bullets, 70
　of paragraphs, 68–69
Info... (CorelPhoto-Paint Image menu), 157
Insert Object... (CorelDraw Edit menu), 48–49
Insert Page... (CorelDraw Layout menu), 50
Intersection (CorelDraw Arrange menu), 50–51
Invert (CorelPhoto-Paint Mask menu), 157–158
Invert (CorelPhoto-Paint Object menu), 158

• J •

JFF file format for imports, 47
JFT file format for imports, 47
JPG file format for imports, 47
justified text, 67

• K •

keywords, 63, 93
kilometers as unit of measurement, 44

• L •

landscape orientation, 65–66
Layers/Objects Roll-Up (CorelPhoto-Paint Object menu), 158–159
Layers Roll-Up (CorelDraw Layout menu), 51–52
Layout menu of CorelDraw
　Delete Page..., 31
　Grid & Scale Setup..., 43–44
　Guidelines Setup..., 45–46
　Insert Page..., 50
　Layers Roll-Up, 51–52
　Page Setup..., 65–66
　Snap To Grid, 44, 97
　Snap To Guidelines, 98
　Snap To Objects, 98
　Styles Roll-Up, 100–101
left-aligning
　paragraphs, 69
　with tabs, 68
　text, 67
Lens Roll-Up (CorelDraw Effects menu), 52–54
light sources in extrudes, 38
lines
　adjusting with Shape tool, 117
　changing to/from curves, 60
　with Dimension lines pencil tool, 119
　drawing tools in CorelPhoto-Paint, 189
　endings with Create Arrow (CorelDraw Special menu), 27
　thickness adjustments with Outline tool, 120–121

varying thickness of, 73–75
line spacing, 14, 67
linking
  objects, 48–49
  with Paste Link option, 72
  updating OLE links, 54–55
Links... (CorelDraw Edit menu), 54–55
Load... (CorelPhoto-Paint Mask menu), 159–160
Load Transparency Mask (CorelPhoto-Paint Mask menu), 159–160
Lotus 1-2-3 file format for imports, 48
Lotus Freelance Plus file format for imports, 48

• M •

Mac-based vector programs
  file format for exports to, 36
  file format for imports from, 48
macros (automatic text string replacement), 112
Magic Wand of CorelPhoto-Paint, 140
magnification
  with lens, 53
  with Zoom tools, 117–118, 184
  See also Zoom
Maintain Aspect option, 84
Mapping filter (CorelPhoto-Paint Effects menu), 152
Marquee Visible (CorelPhoto-Paint Object menu), 160
Mask menu of CorelPhoto-Paint
  All, 126
  Color Mask Roll-Up, 137–138
  Create Transparency Mask, 145–146
  Crop Image, 146–147
  Invert, 157–158
  Load..., 159–160
  Load Transparency Mask, 159–160
  Remove, 171–172
  Remove Transparency Mask, 171–172
  Save, 176
  Save Transparency Mask, 176
masks in CorelDraw
  copying, 142–143
  copying to file, 143
  creating, 21
masks in CorelPhoto-Paint
  adding new areas to, 125
  creating custom-shaped brushes from, 144–145
  creating transparency masks from, 145–146
  cutting, 147
  deleting, 130–131
  inverting, 157
  Pick tools for, 186–187
  removing areas from, 172
  selecting color ranges to protect from change, 137–138
master layers, 51–52
masters, selecting, 96
Maximize Work Area (CorelPhoto-Paint View menu), 160
measurement units
  for CorelDraw, 14
  for CorelPhoto-Paint, 167
memory considerations in CorelDraw
  of creating OLE links to other applications, 55
  of Draw When Moving preference setting, 77
  of opening other applications to create objects, 49
  of performing extrudes, 39
  of roll-ups, 91
  See also speed considerations
Merge Back... (CorelDraw Special menu), 56
Merge (CorelPhoto-Paint Object menu), 160–161
Micrografx Designer
  file format for exports to, 36
  file format for imports from, 48
miles as unit of measurement, 44
millimeters as unit of measurement, 14, 44, 46
miter limit preferences, 76
monitor, calibrating colors on, 18
Mosaic Roll-Up... (CorelDraw File menu), 56–58
Mosaic Roll-Up (CorelPhoto-Paint File menu), 161–162
mouse, setting preferences for right button, 76
mouse pointer, setting preferences for crosshair style in drawing area, 77
moving objects, setting preferences for redrawing, 77

• N •

naming
  documents, 92
  styles, 113–114
nested groups, 45
New (CorelDraw File menu), 58
New (CorelPhoto-Paint File menu), 162–163

New From Template... (CorelDraw Edit menu), 58–59
Node Edit Roll-Up (CorelDraw Shape tool), 59–61
nodes
  adding or deleting, 59–60
  connecting or breaking, 60
  cusp, smooth or symmetrical, 60
  as points or hollow squares, 59
Noise filter (CorelPhoto-Paint Effects menu), 152
nudges, setting preferences for amount of, 75

• O •

Object Data Roll-Up (CorelDraw Object menu), 61–62
Object menu of CorelDraw
  Apply Style, 8–9
  Object Data Roll-Up, 61–62
  Overprint Fill, 64
  Overprint Outline, 64–65
  Revert To Master, 90
  Revert To Style, 89
  Save As Style..., 93–94
  Select Clones, 96
  Select Master, 96
  Update Style..., 113–114
Object menu of CorelPhoto-Paint
  All, 126
  Build Mode, 127–128
  Create, 143–144
  Delete, 147
  Distort, 148–150
  Duplicate, 150
  Flip, 156
  Invert, 158
  Layers/Objects Roll-Up, 158–159
  Marquee Visible, 160
  Merge, 160–161
  Rotate, 174–175
  Skew, 178–179
  Stretch, 180
objects in CorelDraw
  applying lenses for special effects, 52–54
  attaching database information to, 61–62
  cloning, 15–16
  combining, 21
  converting to curves, 23–24
  copying, 25–26
  creating concentric images of, 22
  creating in other applications for linking/embedding, 48–49
  creating of intersection of two other objects, 50–51
  cutting (deleting), 30–31
  extruding (two dimensions into three), 37–39
  grouping, 44–45
  Pick (selecting) tool, 116
  placing inside another object, 72–73
  rearranging stacking order, 63–64
  returning extracted to current drawing, 56
  selecting all, 95
  selecting with spacebar immediately after drawing, 119
  shape modification tool, 116–117
  snapping to, 98
  transforming with precise positioning, 106–110
  trimming overlaps, 110
  twisting, 33–34
  uncombining, 13
  ungrouping, 114
  welding together overlapping, 114–115
  See also complex objects in CorelPhoto-Paint; groups; transformations
objects in CorelPhoto-Paint
  copying, 142–143, 150
  copying to file, 143
  creating from "built" areas, 143–144
  cutting, 147
  deleting, 130–131
  editing and positioning, 158–159
  inverting, 158
  merging to images, 160–161
  rotating, 174–175
  skewing, 178–179
  stretching, 180
  tools for picking, 185–186
odd-even pages, selecting for printing, 83
OLE applications, 54, 55
  PANOSE Font Matching unavailable, 79
100% (no zoom) in CorelPhoto-Paint, 124
Open... (CorelDraw File menu), 62–63
Open (CorelPhoto-Paint File menu), 163–164
Order (CorelDraw Arrange menu), 63–64
orientation (portrait or landscape) selection, 65–66
Outline Pen tools (CorelDraw Tools menu), 120–121

outline view, 115
overlapping objects
    keeping in CorelPhoto-Paint objects and masks, 183–184
    trimming, 110
    welding together, 114–115
overlays in CorelPhoto-Paint, 128–129
Overprint Fill (CorelDraw Object menu), 64
overprinting, 64–65
Overprint Outline (CorelDraw Object menu), 64–65

• P •

page distance, for scaling drawings, 44
page frame selections, 66
page layout selections, 66
PageMaker file format for exports, 36
page outlines, toggle switch for displaying or hiding, 66
pages
    deleting, 31
    inserting additional, 50
Page Setup... (CorelDraw Layout menu), 65–66
page size selection, 65
Paint Brush tools in CorelPhoto-Paint, 189–190
palette
    changing, 20
    changing in CorelPhoto-Paint, 140
PANOSE font matching, 79
PANTONE color-matching systems, 20
Paper Size (CorelPhoto-Paint Image menu), 164–165
Paragraph... (CorelDraw Text menu), 66–70
paragraphs
    with bullets, 69–70
    indenting first lines of, 69
    spacing between, 67
Paragraph text, 9
    changing default text attributes for, 14
    in columns, 41–42
    editing, 32–33
    number of characters per line in envelopes, 78
    spell checking, 98–99
    types of styles for, 94, 101
pasteboards, 52
Paste (CorelDraw Edit menu), 70–71
Paste (CorelPhoto-Paint Edit menu), 165

Paste From File (CorelPhoto-Paint Edit menu), 166
Paste Special command, 54, 55
Paste Special... (CorelDraw Edit menu), 71–72
pasting
    copied objects, 26
    cut objects, 31
patterns
    with CorelDraw Fill tool, 121–122
    with CorelPhoto-Paint Fill tool, 153–155
    customizing in CorelDraw, 28–29
PCC file format for imports, 47
PCD file format for imports, 47
PC Paintbrush file format for exports, 36
PCX extensions, 36
Pen button, 74
Pencil tools (CorelDraw Tools menu), 118–119
pen selection for hand-drawn look, 73–75
perspective
    adding to objects, 5–6
    resetting, 15
Photo-Paint
    changes in version E1, 123
    exiting, 150–151
picas as unit of measurement, 14, 44, 46
Pick tool (CorelDraw Tools menu), 116
PICT file formats for exports, 36
pictures. See images in CorelPhoto-Paint
placing objects with Place button (Transform Roll-Ups), 106–107
PLT extensions, 47
pointed shapes with Create Arrow (CorelDraw Special menu), 27
points as unit of measurement, 14, 44, 46
polygons with CorelPhoto-Paint polygon tool, 185, 190
Polygon tool in CorelPhoto-Paint, 190
portrait or landscape orientation, 65–66
PostScript printers and EPS format for file exports, 36
PostScript Texture fills dialog box, 122
PowerClip (CorelDraw Effects menu), 72–73
PowerLine Roll-Up (CorelDraw Effects menu), 73–75

PowerLines editing, 61
Preferences... (CorelDraw Special menu), 75–80
Preferences... (CorelPhoto-Paint Special menu), 166–167
Presets Roll-Up (CorelDraw Special menu), 80–81
Preview Selected Only (CorelDraw View menu), 82
previews, viewing all or only selected objects, 82
Print... (CorelDraw File menu), 82–85
Print... (CorelPhoto-Paint File menu), 167–170
printers
  calibrating colors on, 18
  CorelDraw settings for, 83
  CorelPhoto-Paint settings for, 168, 171
printer's marks, 84
printing
  and overprinting, 64
  selecting in CorelDraw, 86–87
  selecting in CorelPhoto-Paint, 167–170
Print Merge... (CorelDraw File menu), 86
print previews, 86
Print Setup... (CorelDraw File menu), 86–87
Print Setup... (CorelPhoto-Paint File menu), 170–171
profiling colors (System Color Profile), 17, 18–19
proportional resizing at print time, 84

• *Q* •

quotation mark replacement (typographic for straight), 111

• *R* •

rectangles
  converting to curves, 23–24
  drawing with CorelDraw Rectangle tool, 119
  drawing with CorelPhoto-Paint Rectangle tool, 185
  rounding corners with Shape tool, 117
Rectangle tool (CorelDraw Tools menu), 119
Redo (CorelDraw Edit menu), 87
Refresh (CorelPhoto-Paint Window menu), 171

refreshing screen
  and bitmap resolution, 9, 80
  manually in CorelDraw, 87–88
  manually in CorelPhoto-Paint, 171
  setting preferences for interruptibility, 76
  setting preferences for manual, 77
Refresh Window (CorelDraw View menu), 87–88
registration, overprinting for traps, 64
registration marks, 84, 169
Remove (CorelPhoto-Paint Mask menu), 171–172
Remove From Selection (CorelPhoto-Paint Special menu), 172
Remove Transparency Mask (CorelPhoto-Paint Mask menu), 171–172
Repeat (CorelDraw Edit menu), 88
Replace... (CorelDraw Text menu), 88–89
Resample... (CorelPhoto-Paint Image menu), 172–173
resizing, drawings at print time, 84
resolution
  considerations for bitmaps, 9
  considerations for custom patterns, 28–29
Restore To Checkpoint (CorelPhoto-Paint Edit menu), 173
reversed images, 84
Revert To Master (CorelDraw Object menu), 90
Revert To Style (CorelDraw Object menu), 89
RGB colors, 20
ribbon bar preferences, 77
right-aligning
  paragraphs, 69
  with tabs, 68
  text, 67
Roll-Ups (CorelDraw View menu), 90–91
Rotate (CorelPhoto-Paint Image menu), 174–175
Rotate (CorelPhoto-Paint Object menu), 174–175
rotation
  for blends, 11
  in CorelPhoto-Paint, 174–175
  of curves, 60
  with precise adjustments in CorelDraw, 107–108
  with precise adjustments in CorelPhoto-Paint, 148–150
  resetting, 15

of text to graphic object's outline, 40–41
rulers
for adjusting guidelines, 45
for setting tab stops, 68
Rulers (CorelDraw View menu), 92
Rulers (CorelPhoto-Paint View menu), 175

• S •

saturation of images in CorelPhoto-Paint, 133
Save As... (CorelPhoto-Paint File menu), 175–176
Save As Style... (CorelDraw Object menu), 93–94
Save (CorelDraw File menu), 92–93
Save (CorelPhoto-Paint File menu), 175–176
Save (CorelPhoto-Paint Mask menu), 176
Save Transparency Mask (CorelPhoto-Paint Mask menu), 176
saving
importance of frequent, 80
text objects as ASCII text files, 36–37
scale adjustments, 43–44
scaling
PowerLine proportions, 74
with precise adjustments in CorelDraw, 108
with precise adjustments in CorelPhoto-Paint, 149
resetting, 15
Scan Gallery, file format for imports from, 48
scanners
calibrating colors on, 18
pulling images into CorelPhoto-Paint, 124–125
screen. *See* refreshing screen
Screen Dithering (CorelPhoto-Paint View menu), 177
Screen/Menu Help... (CorelDraw Help menu), 94
Search For Help On (CorelDraw Help menu), 94–95
Select All (CorelDraw Edit menu), 95
Select Clones (CorelDraw Object menu), 96
Select (CorelPhoto-Paint Special menu), 177
Select Master (CorelDraw Object menu), 96
Select Partial Area... (CorelPhoto-Paint File menu), 177–178
sentences, capitalizing first letters of, 111
Separate (CorelDraw Arrange menu), 96–97
separations, 85, 169
Shape tool
in CorelPhoto-Paint, 190
Node Edit Roll-Up, 59–61
on CorelDraw Tools menu, 116–117
Sharpen filter (CorelPhoto-Paint Effects menu), 152–153
sharpen tool of CorelPhoto-Paint, 191
Shift+key combinations in CorelDraw
Shift+F1 for Screen/Menu Help..., 94
Shift+F8 for Paragraph text tool, 120
Shift+F9 for Wireframe, 115
Shift+F11 for Uniform Fill dialog box, 122
Shift+F12 for Outline Pen color dialog box, 121
Shift+PgUp/PgDn keys for rearranging stacking order of objects, 63–64
Shift+key combinations in CorelPhoto-Paint
Shift+F4 for Tile Vertically, 180
Shift+F5 for Cascade, 129–130
Shift+F6 for Fill Roll-Up, 153–156
Show Grid, 44, 97
sizing
with precise adjustments in CorelDraw, 108–109
with precise adjustments in CorelPhoto-Paint, 149
Skew (CorelPhoto-Paint Object menu), 178–179
skews
with precise adjustments in CorelDraw, 109–110
with precise adjustments in CorelPhoto-Paint, 149–150, 178–179
resetting, 15
"smart" quotation marks (typographic instead of straight), 111
smear tool of CorelPhoto-Paint, 191
smooth nodes, 60
smudge tool of CorelPhoto-Paint, 191
Snap To Grid (CorelDraw Layout menu), 44, 97
Snap To Guidelines (CorelDraw Layout menu), 98

Snap To Objects (CorelDraw Layout menu), 98
Soften filter (CorelPhoto-Paint Effects menu), 153
spacebar
  for Pick tool, 116
  for selection of just-drawn objects, 119
  for toggling between tools, 119
spacing, between characters, words, lines or paragraphs, 67
special effects
  cloning, 16–17
  copying, 24–25
  recording, saving, and applying, 80–81
  saving as styles, 93–94
  specifying anchor nodes for blends, 12
Special filter (CorelPhoto-Paint Effects menu), 153
Special menu of CorelDraw
  Create Arrow..., 27–28
  Create Pattern..., 28–29
  Create Symbol..., 29–30
  Extract..., 36–37
  Merge Back..., 56
  Preferences..., 75–80
  Presets Roll-Up, 80–81
  Symbols Roll-Up, 101–102
Special menu of CorelPhoto-Paint
  Add To Selection, 125–126
  Color Tolerance, 140–141
  Create Brush, 144–145
  Preferences..., 166–167
  Remove From Selection, 172
  Select, 177
  XOR Selection, 183–184
speed considerations in CorelDraw
  of bitmap resolution, 9, 80
  of Draw When Moving preference setting, 77
  of extrude minimum facet size, 78
  for greeking of text, 78
  of on-screen color correction, 17
  of outline view, 115
  for viewing all or only selected objects in Full-Screen Preview, 82
  See also memory considerations
speed considerations in CorelPhoto-Paint, Color Correction, 134
Speedometer button, 74
Spell Checker... (CorelDraw Text menu), 98–99
Split Channels To (CorelPhoto-Paint Image menu), 179–180
splitting blends, 12–13
squares, rounding corners with Shape tool, 117
Square tool in CorelPhoto-Paint, 190
status line, 116, 120
  preferences, 77
Straighten Text (CorelDraw Text menu), 99–100
Stretch (CorelPhoto-Paint Object menu), 180
stretching
  in CorelDraw, 15
  in CorelPhoto-Paint, 180
styles
  applying, 8–9
  applying and managing in templates, 100–101
  hotkeys for, 101
  predefined for layouts, 85
  reverting to original for object, 89
  updating or renaming, 113–114
Styles Roll-Up (CorelDraw Layout menu), 100–101
symbols
  adding categories, 30
  creating, 29–30
  displaying library of, 101–102
  selecting for bullets, 69–70
  TrueType fonts for, 29, 30
Symbols Roll-Up (CorelDraw Special menu), 101–102
symmetrical nodes, 60
synonyms from Thesaurus, 104–105
System Color Profile
  in CorelDraw, 17, 18–19
  in CorelPhoto-Paint, 134–137

• T •

Tab settings, 68
templates
  creating drawings from, 58–59
  for styles, 100–101
text
  adjusting spacing with Shape tool, 117
  aligning to baseline, 7–8
  automatic string replacement, 112
  changing attributes of characters, 13–14
  finding, 39–40
  finding and replacing, 88–89
  fitting baselines to graphic object's outline, 40–41
  formatting options, 103–104
  restoring to baseline, 99–100

separating original fitted from intermediate, 96
setting preferences for edits, greeking, and so on, 78–79
spell checking, 98–99
Text menu of CorelDraw
　Align to Baseline, 7–8
　Character..., 13–14
　Edit Text..., 32–33
　Find..., 39–40
　Fit Text To Path, 40–41
　Frame..., 41–42
　Paragraph..., 66–70
　Replace..., 88–89
　Spell Checker..., 98–99
　Straighten Text, 99–100
　Text Roll-Up, 103–104
　Thesaurus..., 104–105
　Type Assist..., 111–112
text objects
　converting to curves, 23–24
　saving as ASCII text files, 36–37
Text Roll-Up (CorelDraw Text menu), 103–104, 120
Text tool in CorelDraw, 120
Text tool in CorelPhoto-Paint, 191
Texture fills dialog box in CorelDraw, 122
texture fills in CorelPhoto-Paint, 155–156
textures, applying in CorelPhoto-Paint, 128–129
TGA file format for imports, 47
Thesaurus... (CorelDraw Text menu), 104–105
three-dimensional effects
　in CorelPhoto-Paint transformations, 153
　with extrudes, 37–39
TIF file format for imports, 47
Tile Horizontally (CorelPhoto-Paint Windows menu), 180
Tile Vertically (CorelPhoto-Paint Windows menu), 180
toggles, 9
Tone filter (CorelPhoto-Paint Effects menu), 153
tone map of images in CorelPhoto-Paint, adjusting, 133–134
Toolbox (CorelDraw View menu), 105
Toolbox (CorelPhoto-Paint View menu), 182–183
tools in CorelPhoto-Paint
　for cloning, 192
　for creating geometric shapes, 190
　Fill, 191
　for line drawing, 189

　mask pickers, 186–187
　modes of, 177
　object pickers, 185–186
　Paint Brushes, 189–190
　selecting settings for, 181–182
　for smears, smudges, sharpening, contrast, and color adjustments, 191–192
　Text, 191
　toggling between visible and invisible, 182–183
　Tool Settings Roll-Up, 181–182
　for undoing, 188
　Zoom, 187–188
Tools menu of CorelDraw
　Ellipse tool, 119–120
　Fill tools, 121–122
　Outline Pen tools, 120–121
　Pencil tools, 118–119
　Pick tool, 116
　Rectangle tool, 119
　Shape tool, 116–117
　Text tool, 120
　Zoom tools, 117–118
　See also icons
transferring files (exporting), 35–36
transformations
　bitmaps at low resolution for, 9
　clearing, 15
Transformations filter (CorelPhoto-Paint Effects menu), 153
Transform Roll-Ups (CorelDraw Effects menu), 106–110
transparency effect with lens, 53
transparency masks in CorelPhoto-Paint
　editing and positioning, 158
　inverting, 157
　loading, 159–160
　removing from current image, 171–172
　saving, 176
traps, 64, 65
　with AutoTrapping, 85
Trim (CorelDraw Arrange menu), 110
TrueType fonts
　converting to Type 1, 85
　for symbols, 29, 30
TRUMATCH color-matching system, 20
Tutorial (CorelDraw Help menu), 110–111
twisting objects
　in CorelDraw, 33–34
　in CorelPhoto-Paint, 151–153
Type Assist... (CorelDraw Text menu), 111–112

• U •

Undo (CorelDraw Edit menu), 76, 112–113
Undo (CorelPhoto-Paint Edit menu), 183
Undo tools in CorelPhoto-Paint, 188
Ungroup (CorelDraw Arrange menu), 114
Uniform Colors (RBG model palette), 20
Uniform Fill dialog box, 122
units of measurement
   selecting for CorelDraw, 14
   selecting for CorelPhoto-Paint, 167
Update Style... (CorelDraw Object menu), 113–114

• V •

vanishing points, Xs as, 6
vector programs (Mac-based)
   file format for exports to, 36
   file format for imports from, 48
Ventura Publisher (CorelVentura)
   file format for exports to, 36
vertical alignment, 7
   of bullets, 70
   to gridlines, 44
   with guidelines, 45
View menu of CorelDraw
   Bitmaps, 9–10
   Color Correction, 17
   Color Palette, 19–21
   Full-Screen Preview, 42–43
   Preview Selected Only, 82
   Refresh Window, 87–88
   Roll-Ups, 90–91
   Rulers, 92
   Toolbox, 105
   Wireframe, 115
View menu of CorelPhoto-Paint
   Canvas Roll-Up, 128–129
   Color Correction, 134–135
   Color Roll-Up, 138–140
   Fill Roll-Up, 153–156
   Full-Screen Preview, 157
   Maximize Work Area, 160
   Rulers, 175
   Screen Dithering, 177
   Toolbox, 182–183
   Zoom, 184
   Zoom To Fit, 184–185
Visible (Wireframe view option), 9

• W •

waveforms, 33–34
Weld (CorelDraw Arrange menu), 114–115
wildcards
   disallowed in replace strings, 89
   in File Name boxes, 63, 164
Window menu of CorelPhoto-Paint, Refresh, 171
windows, setting preferences for scrolling, 76
Windows menu of CorelPhoto-Paint
   Arrange Icons, 126–127
   Cascade, 129–130
   Tile Horizontally, 180
   Tile Vertically, 180
Wireframe (CorelDraw View menu), 115
WMF extensions, 36
Word for Windows
   file format for exports to, 36
   maintaining OLE links with, 54–55
WordPerfect
   file format for exports to, 36
   file format for imports from, 48
words
   spacing between, 67
   synonyms from Thesaurus, 104–105
work areas in CorelPhoto-Paint, maximizing, 160
world distance for scaling drawings, 44
WPG extensions, 36

• X •

Xs as vanishing points, 6

• Z •

Zoom (CorelPhoto-Paint View menu), 184
Zoom To Fit (CorelPhoto-Paint View menu), 184–185
Zoom tools
   in CorelDraw, 117–118
   in CorelPhoto-Paint, 187–188
   for finding "lost" pasted objects, 26
   for "unzooming" in CorelPhoto-Paint, 124

IDG BOOKS WORLDWIDE REGISTRATION CARD

RETURN THIS REGISTRATION CARD FOR FREE CATALOG

Title of this book: CORELDRAW! 5 FOR DUMMIES QR

My overall rating of this book: ❏ Very good [1] ❏ Good [2] ❏ Satisfactory [3] ❏ Fair [4] ❏ Poor [5]

How I first heard about this book:

❏ Found in bookstore; name: [6] ❏ Book review: [7]
❏ Advertisement: [8] ❏ Catalog: [9]
❏ Word of mouth; heard about book from friend, co-worker, etc.: [10] ❏ Other: [11]

What I liked most about this book:

What I would change, add, delete, etc., in future editions of this book:

Other comments:

Number of computer books I purchase in a year: ❏ 1 [12] ❏ 2-5 [13] ❏ 6-10 [14] ❏ More than 10 [15]

I would characterize my computer skills as: ❏ Beginner [16] ❏ Intermediate [17] ❏ Advanced [18] ❏ Professional [19]

I use ❏ DOS [20] ❏ Windows [21] ❏ OS/2 [22] ❏ Unix [23] ❏ Macintosh [24] ❏ Other: [25] _____
(please specify)

I would be interested in new books on the following subjects:
(please check all that apply, and use the spaces provided to identify specific software)

❏ Word processing: [26] ❏ Spreadsheets: [27]
❏ Data bases: [28] ❏ Desktop publishing: [29]
❏ File Utilities: [30] ❏ Money management: [31]
❏ Networking: [32] ❏ Programming languages: [33]
❏ Other: [34]

I use a PC at (please check all that apply): ❏ home [35] ❏ work [36] ❏ school [37] ❏ other: [38]

The disks I prefer to use are ❏ 5.25 [39] ❏ 3.5 [40] ❏ other: [41]

I have a CD ROM: ❏ yes [42] ❏ no [43]

I plan to buy or upgrade computer hardware this year: ❏ yes [44] ❏ no [45]

I plan to buy or upgrade computer software this year: ❏ yes [46] ❏ no [47]

Name: _____ **Business title:** [48] _____
Type of Business: [49]
Address (❏ home [50] ❏ work [51]/Company name: _____)
Street/Suite#
City [52]/**State** [53]/**Zipcode** [54]: _____ **Country** [55] _____

❏ **I liked this book!**
You may quote me by name in future IDG Books Worldwide promotional materials.

My daytime phone number is _____

IDG BOOKS
THE WORLD OF COMPUTER KNOWLEDGE

❏ **YES!**
Please keep me informed about IDG's World of Computer Knowledge. Send me the latest IDG Books catalog.

NO POSTAGE
NECESSARY
IF MAILED
IN THE
UNITED STATES

BUSINESS REPLY MAIL
FIRST CLASS MAIL   PERMIT NO. 2605   SAN MATEO, CALIFORNIA

IDG Books Worldwide
155 Bovet Rd
San Mateo CA 94402-9833